THE
Clash of Ideas

ESSAYS IN HONOUR OF
PATRICK LYNCH

Edited by Miriam Hederman

GILL AND MACMILLAN

Published in Ireland by
Gill and Macmillan Ltd
Goldenbridge
Dublin 8
with associated companies in
Auckland, Delhi, Gaborone, Hamburg, Harare, Hong Kong,
Johannesburg, Kuala Lumpur, Lagos, London, Manzini,
Melbourne, Mexico City, Nairobi, New York, Singapore, Tokyo
© Asa Briggs, Peter Froggatt, John Kenneth Galbraith, Miriam Hederman,
Patrick Honohan, Richard Kearney, John Maguire, Terry Stewart, 1988
Print origination
Graphic Plan, Dublin
Printed by Criterion Press, Dublin

British Cataloguing in Publication Data
The clash of ideas: essays in honour of Patrick Lynch.
1. Humanities
1. Hederman, Miriam
001.3

ISBN 0-7171-1596-8

Contents

'An essential condition of progress is
the desire for change,
a resentment of stagnation,
a willingness to depart from obsolete ideas,
leadership with a consistent sense of direction
a healthy, courageous and constructive public opinion;
above all, concern for the preservation or reform, where necessary,
of every institution which the community has established as
an instrument of achieving national and economic advance.
Ireland has unused human and material resources, but there must be a
change in the attitudes towards using them. More than anything else, new
ideas count in the long run — provided they are the right ones.'

Patrick Lynch, 'The Economics of Independence —
Some Unsettled Questions of Irish Economics'
Administration 7/2, Summer 1959

Acknowledgment

The publishers acknowledge the generous assistance
of Allied Irish Banks
in supporting the publication of this book.

Foreword

IN a BBC television programme of some ten years back that was later broadcast from Dublin, I asserted the exceptional aptitude of the Scots and the Jews as regards economics. But I added that all of the great races had produced economists — with the possible exception of the Irish. This last circumstance I attributed to the preference of Irish intellectuals for more appealing, graceful and civilised concerns.

As I had hoped, my comment brought a vigorous Irish response; I was rewarded with a list of numerous Irish economists, some of nearly impeccable anonymity. But most of all, and with varying expressions of correction, amusement and indignation, there was mention of Patrick Lynch. In response I confessed my grave omission. I hope that this brief comment, in the context of a book which deserves great success and wide currency, will compensate for that omission.

I've known Paddy Lynch for thirty or more years. And I've known also of his incredibly diverse and useful career. I know of economists, many in fact, who along with teaching have ventured into public service, corporate business counselling or some other enterprise in the field of philanthropy or social service. A colleague of mine once turned up in intimate association with one of the more spectacular international frauds of our time, which did some damage to his academic career. Excepting only the last, Paddy Lynch has engaged in the course of one lifetime in not one but all of these activities and more. He has been a public servant, a lecturer and professor, a banker, the guiding force of an airline, a participant in numerous investigatory bodies and commissions, an advocate of civilised decencies abroad and at home, and I can think of no one quite like him in our profession. Certainly he is at the opposite pole from the careful scholar who commutes from passive domesticity to equally passive mathematical models, avoiding all intrusion of reality on the comfortable world he regards as a manifestation of true science.

We all know that Ireland is a country with serious, even grave, economic problems. The transition from elementary agriculture to modern industrial forms was difficult here, made more so by the presence of more richly or spaciously endowed countries west and east. But what has not been so widely recognised is the extraordinary quality—in intelligence, devotion to the public interest and absolute personal integrity—of the group of leaders Ireland has had contending with her problems. In their absence the prospect would have been truly grim. I've known these men, many of them, over the last third of a century. It is they who have drawn me repeatedly to Dublin. First among them has been Patrick Lynch.

This is my view, but I venture it with exceptional confidence, for it has also the support of all this distinguished group of friends. It is nice, on occasion, to reflect the fully accepted opinion.

Contributors

Miriam Hederman, writer, broadcaster and barrister-at-law is a graduate of University College Dublin and was awarded a doctorate in Political Science from Trinity College Dublin. She was Chairman of the Commission on Taxation, 1980-85, and is currently Chairman of the Commission on Health Funding. She has been a member of the National Economic and Social Council since 1984 and is Chairman of the Irish Committee of the European Cultural Foundation.

Patrick Honohan, a graduate of University College Dublin and the London School of Economics, is a lecturer in economics at UCD and is currently on leave of absence at the World Bank, Washington DC. He was Economic Adviser to Dr Garret FitzGerald as Taoiseach.

Asa Briggs graduated from Sidney Sussex College Cambridge where he was awarded a double first in history. In 1976 he became Provost of Worcester College Oxford and since 1978 has been Chancellor of the Open University. He is currently President of the British Social History Society. Lord Briggs was made a Life Peer in 1976.

John Maguire, after graduating from University College Dublin, received his D. Phil. degree from Oxford University where he was a Research Fellow of Nuffield College from 1973 to 1975. He taught politics at UCD until 1978, and since then he has been Professor of Social Theory and Institutions at University College Cork.

Peter Froggatt, a native of Belfast, graduated in medicine from Trinity College Dublin and specialised in industrial medicine. He was Dean of the Faculty of Medicine at Queen's University Belfast 1971-1976, and Vice-Chancellor of the University 1976-1986. He is now a director of several public companies and a Pro-Chancellor of Trinity College Dublin.

Richard Kearney was born in Cork, graduated from University College Dublin and McGill University Montreal and was awarded a Ph.D. from the University of Paris. He lectures in philosophy at UCD. He is the author of several books on Irish culture and European philosophy and was co-editor of *The Crane Bag;* at present he co-edits *The Irish Review.*

Terry Stewart graduated in economics at Queen's University Belfast. After twelve years in the Northern Ireland Ministry of Commerce and other public appointments in the Republic, he became a permanent official of the Commission of the European Communities in 1979, and since January 1987 he had been Head of the Commission Office, based in Dublin.

Introduction: Patrick Lynch

THE title of this tribute to Patrick Lynch is a quotation from his writing and is used to describe a Festschrift of an unusual kind. The 'clash' in question is the generation of energy which occurs when ideas meet, bounce off each other and renew the participants, writers and readers, as a result of the experience. It is not the ritual confrontation beloved of manipulators of public debate. Patrick Lynch has been noted for his avoidance of conflict when problems can be resolved through other means. But he has not avoided the unpalatable parting of the ways when principles are so deeply divided that practice becomes irreconcilable. Living together despite deep divisions is a test of our civilisation.

The inspiration for the book came neither from former students nor from present colleagues of this most unusual person, but from someone who has never met Patrick Lynch.* It is a tribute to the depth and relevance of his writings, to his contribution to the service of the public good, his teaching and, above all, his combination of positive comment and rigorous analysis.

*Donal O'Brolchain has spent most of his working life in the public service and is now Managing Director of Procyon Informatics, a Dublin-based software engineering company. He believes that creating a common prosperity calls for a rethink of our attitudes to change, our sense of community and our view of personal effort. In this, he has been inspired by Patrick Lynch—a person who has, for the past forty years, kept closely in touch with the life of his own times, and has proposed new directions for areas as diverse as civil service reform, educational investment, social policy and the use of scientific know-how for development.

1

Instead of praising the accomplishments of the subjects, the collected essays take them as a springboard from which the writers have tried to make a contribution for coming generations. The contributors differ widely in background, age and philosophy. In no way do they purport to interpret what Patrick Lynch himself would say on their particular subject. Their brief was to use their experience so that the areas which they know best (and in which Professor Lynch was a significant actor in his time) could be publicly discussed in order to prepare and improve them for the future. Each author has accepted the challenge of emulating rather than praising or even commenting on 'Paddy Lynch's' achievements. In view of this self-denial a brief word is needed here about the context in which Professor Lynch must be regarded as an important figure.

The curriculum vitae of the subject reveals a remarkable diversity of activity and interests and a sustained dedication to public service in different guises.

Eleven years as civil servant and adviser to the head of Government was followed by twenty-eight as lecturer and professor of economics in University College Dublin. This long period coincided with a steady stream of extra-curricular activities through which he guided public enquiries into education, research and technology and was responsible for ensuring that at least some of the findings would be implemented.

As Chairman of Aer Lingus from 1954 to 1975, Patrick Lynch presided over the development of one of the more successful state interventions in economic life and a dynamic state-sponsored company. As a member of the Board of the Provincial Bank, later of Allied Irish Banks from 1959 until he retired as Deputy Chairman of A.I.B. in 1984, he participated in the rationalisation and vigorous growth of the Irish banks and saw the private financial sector learn to compete successfully on the international scene. The man who acted as Chairman of the Irish Anti-Apartheid Movement in the seventies, served on the Senate of the National University of Ireland and was Treasurer of the Royal Irish Academy, touched the lives of many who never knew of his existence. His influence has been described as 'more shadowy and possibly more pervasive' than that of many of his talented but more flamboyant contemporaries.

All years are important but the year in which this book is published is a critical one for Ireland and the wider European community of which she is part. There are grave problems which threaten the social cohesion of our countries. They are soluble but only if tackled in a positive way and with popular support. If pessimism and even cynicism are prevalent their causes have to be addressed. If either general hopelessness or over-optimistic euphoria is widespread we will never solve our difficulties. Hence the relevance of someone who has been consistently supportive and unflinchingly realistic.

Patrick Lynch can only inspire an outward-looking view of the world in which we live. A political economist of wide vision, he is sometimes used by the OECD as a 'human resource'. He is the sole Irish member of 'The Club of Rome'.

This Club of Rome is, perhaps, one aspect of his fruitful and diversified career that needs some explanation for those readers who find the term unfamiliar. It is the name of a select and informal association of individuals which began in 1968 but was subsequently chartered in Switzerland; its membership of one hundred was spread across the world. Conceived as a catalyst group that would tackle the problems which beset mankind and stimulate research and discussion 'to understand better the workings of the world as a finite system' it had a small secretariat and neither staff nor formal budget.

The very concept of a hundred people, each an expert in his or her own country in some discipline of learning, working together to improve the quality of *thinking* about issues which affect this and coming generations, is unusual for us. Yet these people, many of whom would be proudly hailed as intellectuals in their own societies, went further, aiming to 'provoke a dialogue with political decision-makers, industrialists, academics and many groups in many places to arouse appreciation of ... the need to consider new policies, attitudes and courses of action to ensure the continuity of mankind and to cultivate a new humanism conducive to world peace, social justice and individual self-fulfilment.'

A combination of American, European and Asian methodology, philosophy and concern produced in 1972 a report to the Club, 'Limits to Growth', described as a first hesitant step towards a new understanding of our world. This provoked quite violent reactions—both positive and negative—but the sponsors were not only unrepentant but proud. The attention of decision-makers was directed to essential problems which can be properly understood only in the context of 'the world system as a whole'. The exercise was destined to blow minds off traditional courses so that national, regional, sectoral and political issues would no longer be addressed as though they existed in isolation wards.

Some of the forecasts made in work commissioned by the Club may be wildly far off the mark. The importance, as stressed by the members, is that planners are now encouraged, and indeed warned, to include social, cultural and 'quality' developments in measuring the effectiveness of their proposals. The era of Gross National Product as the best measurement of growth and progress was brought to an end.

The Club was itself to remain small, but not detached from public concern. It was to provoke debate but to remain free from political affiliation. It was to see similar movements spring up in many countries and then fade into the background.

4

It seems fitting that Patrick Lynch contributed to such a group. The false alternative between local (or national) and international concern and activity is not part of his philosophy. Nor is it true of people in Derry or Dublin who subscribe generously, time and time again, whether the cause be famine in Africa or a special need at home. If a mind is both open and generous it can contribute to more than one issue. And if its capacity was ample to begin with, it will be increased as it responds to other minds with different views. Too many of us perhaps forget the lesson of the biblical talent.

The role of 'thinker' had not been considered particularly important in recent Irish history. 'Thought' has been considered the contrary of 'action' and 'action' has, unfortunately for all of us, been frequently unaccompanied by any serious thought. The message quietly passed to such of his students as were prepared to receive it by Professor Lynch was that 'thought' was not only necessary but capable of development and a requisite for action.

The perception of being at the mercy of vast, alien and hostile forces is not confined to Ireland or even to small open economies. Commentators from other countries who are free to express their misgivings lament the growing power of multinational companies, state control, international bankers or whatever antagonist seems to thwart their personal strategy for a good life for themselves and their sector.

The emphasis on an external conspiracy produces a particularly unhappy mix when it is accepted by people whose humanist, Judaeo-Christian culture has emphasised the importance of the individual and his or her personal responsibility. Civilisations which exalt the destiny of the people or race as a whole can cope with such perceived threats—indeed, they are used as a bond to keep the population united. In the context of the European tradition, however, problems which are described as overwhelming

5

and as being orchestrated from outside can lead to paralysis, division and failure to achieve.

The counter-heresy, which encourages us to wait for and follow the leader who will right all wrongs, dooms us to disappointment and, strangely enough, can also lead to paralysis, division and failure to achieve.

Whether the catch-cry is reds under the bed or capitalism under the covers, there is a very real danger that it will be used as an excuse to persecute some misguided individual who goes against the common enthusiasm and as a substitute for action where action is most needed.

Patrick Lynch preferred to build with the materials to hand rather than lament the absence of more suitable soil. He helped to solve the problems of the fifties and of the sixties and it is our good fortune that he is with us to cope with those of the eighties.

The subjects taken for discussion in this tribute are not exhaustive of those which might have been covered but they raise some of the most important issues we have to resolve. What is the role of those who make and those who administer policy in the public and private sectors? How might we improve our performance? What kind of community do we want to be? How can we influence the European Community to evolve as we believe it should?

It is hoped that the contributions will generate constructive debate since they are both positive and diverse. Some of them state accepted precepts in a new context. Others are likely to be controversial because they reject the most widely-held views of how society ought to work. There has been no attempt to achieve consensus or balance, or to produce any of the ingredients which may be desirable in other fora but which would reduce a study such as this to a mess of blancmange, unworthy of the person it is designed to honour.

Miriam Hederman
May 1988

PATRICK HONOHAN

1. The Role of the Adviser and the Evolution of the Public Service

AT the beginning of the new decade of the 1980s, few if any foresaw just how deep and how protracted the economic crisis would be. Many felt that fiscal expansion had been overdone; that an unpopular but feasible correction in the public finances was now necessary. But most people thought that a few years of belt tightening, even if exacerbated by the second oil crisis, would be enough to restore balance and allow a resumption of the modest but acceptable levels of growth that had been the norm for two decades. But growth did not return and, despite the retrenchment, the public finances did not come even close to balance. Some lowering of living standards in this period was anticipated, if borrowing was to be brought under control; but the decline was much steeper than the degree of fiscal improvement gained. After seven years the economy was employing far fewer workers—aggregate employment fell in each year—to produce scarcely any more output. Unemployment soared in an unprecedented manner.

There are unresolved issues of economic analysis and interpretation about this period, but the experience also raises fundamental questions about the capacity of our political and administrative system. Why was the extent of the crisis not appreciated in advance? Are there policies which can reverse the malaise, and if so why have they not been adopted? Is the permanent administration willing to map out a new direction?

7

Some knowledge of how strategic economic planning has been carried out in recent years can help towards an understanding of these important issues. The following paragraphs are offered as such a contribution. As a former participant in the administrative system rather than an expert or professional observer of it, I should be wary of advancing proposals. Nevertheless there are points worth contributing to a debate on institutional reform which has become urgent.

We may recall the textbook classification of the role of the economic system, which, we are told, determines *how much* of *what* is produced *for whom*, and *how*. The role of government has come to embody aspects of each of these functions. *How much* government spending or borrowing should there be? *What* should the spending be on? In its re-distributive role the government decides *for whom* the fruits of economic activity will be harvested, and the legislative and regulatory environment may strongly influence *how*. These four categories are thus suitable headings under which to carry on our discussion.

HOW MUCH

The Fiscal Problem

Governments of the 1980s have been preoccupied with the deficit in the government's accounts and the rapid rise in external debt. *How much* more can government afford to spend than it receives in taxation and other revenue; and when an acceptable target for this deficit has been established, how can it be achieved? These questions have absorbed most of the intellectual energy of government and its advisers since the beginning of the decade. We cannot begin to understand the policy process without a clear picture of how this crucial policy problem has been analysed and understood.

It is not so long since there was a straightforward answer to the question of 'how much'. Until the early 1970s the unanimous message of civil servants, academics and bankers was clear-cut; no deficit should be planned on current account, but borrowing was permissible for productive capital investment. It was Professor Lynch who, as Economic Adviser to the then Taoiseach, John A. Costello, developed the concept of a separate Capital Account in the Budget as introduced in 1950. At a stroke, this device provided a way for governments anxious to address the development needs of the economy, apparently without risking insolvency or inflation. As a growing commercial firm need not finance all investment out of current earnings, so too, ran the consensus view, the Irish government should rely on borrowed funds to exploit growth opportunities requiring capital.

Like any simple rule, the capital budget had its limitations as a guide for policy. Evident conceptually, these also began to be relevant in a practical way by the early 1970s or even before: as early as 1965 debt servicing costs exceeded 3 per cent of GNP. On the one hand, not all capital investment generated the tax revenue which would have been required to service the debt which had been assumed to pay for it. A programme of borrowing for just about anything that could conceivably be called 'capital' requires increasing rates of tax to finance the debt servicing. Because of low real interest rates and a buoyant economy the underlying unsustainability of such an approach did not impose severe pressures at first, but it rapidly proved disastrous in the changed conditions after 1973.

On the other hand the absolute prohibition on current borrowing could be damaging to the economy hit by an unfavourable temporary shock: and could in such circumstances be justified only by the self-discipline that such an automatic rule generated for governments. As it turned out,

9

by the time such a shock came the balanced budget rule had been broken and no longer governed policy.

Rather than tracing the course of the public finances in the 1970s along what is by now a well-trodden track, we jump forward to consider the situation facing governments in the early 1980s, and the advice they were given from different sources. The fiscal situation can be summarised by four facts:

—The state's debt grew faster than national output year by year, reaching very high levels by international standards, with the foreign component approaching half of the total debt.

—The current budget deficit (which should have been zero on the old Lynch-Whitaker rule), reached a record figure of about eight per cent of GNP by 1982 and remained around that figure for the following five years. Total Exchequer borrowing peaked in 1981 and had been reined in six years later, but only to a fairly modest extent.

—Demographic and other pressures impinged on public spending. A sharp decline in employment from 1980 resulted in much greater demands on the social welfare system and, combined with a sharp increase in the value of most payments during 1980-82, contributed to a rapid increase in social welfare spending. This increase alone was equal in size to the current deficit. An even greater increase in spending was recorded under the category of interest payments, partly attributable to a worldwide jump in rates of interest, partly to the ever growing debt.

—There was a massive increase (by about one-third) in the burden of taxation, especially between 1979 and 1984, but this was insufficient, in face of the expenditure increases, to balance the books.

The Diagnoses

What analysis and advice did government receive in these

10

circumstances? Some points were beyond dispute: no one could deny that, if the rate of increase in its debt were maintained, the government's ability to borrow on international capital markets would soon be brought into question. But it would be a mistake to suppose that there was unanimity among advisers on what exactly was happening and what the solution might be.

One oversimplified view enjoyed an early vogue, and was, I believe, influential in determining the course of policy between 1981 and 1984. According to this view the Government's overspending was closely matched by national overspending, as reflected in the balance of international payments, which had increased in line with the Government's borrowing. Accordingly the task facing the Government was a mechanical one with limited adverse consequences: if the Government's overspending could be reduced—by whatever means— the impact would be on national spending, and not on production. It was held by many that the expansion of the Government's deficit had created jobs abroad rather than at home. If so, then by an argument of symmetry, the elimination of that deficit need have little effect on jobs at home.

There were four policy implications of this position. First, expenditure cuts involving public sector job losses should be avoided. After all, the theory stated that the needed financial adjustment could be accomplished without much adverse effect on overall employment, so why impose unnecessary disruption? Second, since it takes time to identify with precision the sources of waste in Government spending programmes, the immediate need for balancing the budget could just as well be achieved by short-term increases in taxation while the waste was being rooted out. Third, since the impact was to be on spending, it would be important to have a fair distribution of the reduction in spending power: the least well off must be protected. Fourth, because the nation's financial problems could be traced back to the time when the Lynch-Whitaker rule had been broken—resulting in excessive national as well as public overspending—the task of correction would only be complete when the current budget deficit had been eliminated.

Though caricatured here, I think that something along these lines reflected the dominant view in official circles in 1981. So far as employment was concerned, the key consideration was competitiveness, in which neither government spending nor taxation played a significant role by comparison with the potential of pay restraint. It would be wrong to deny that some advisers pointed out that employment could be seriously affected by fiscal contraction, at least in the short-term, as national spending power fell. Others worried about the adverse effects of taxation on competitiveness and asserted that a contractionary stance on public expenditure—especially, but not only, in regard to public service pay — was the best way to curb inflation and thereby improve national competitiveness. But these were muted voices by comparison with the clarion to call to balance the budget, by whatever means.

In attempting to understand how this view became predominant it is important to bear in mind the collegial nature of cabinet government. All members of government are exposed to the views of the civil service, of the various advisory bodies, of party colleagues and of the pressure groups. But each member of the cabinet also has independent sources and other influences on his thinking, which are often likely to carry more weight than the formal documents. Because of this diversity of influences, the collective government 'view' on complex issues of central importance will rarely coincide wholly with the opinion held by any individual minister, either before or after discussion, nor with the views of the permanent officials. Diverse political pressures also enter into the picture, and it would require considerable intellectual sophistication to prevent these from contaminating analytical discussion.

Prominent professional economists—several of them close to Ministers—had been arguing for years that government was spending far too much. By 1981, this theme was generally accepted by the media, and found comparatively few dissidents. Nevertheless spending cuts were slow to come. Although it would definitely be wrong to attribute a high-tax lobby to the civil service, I think that it is not unfair to say that the emphasis in official thinking (which I shared) at this period was probably more on over-borrowing than on overspending. We will return to this point later. It was immediate political pressures rather than any intellectual argument that resulted in the choice falling on tax increases rather than spending reductions. In short, it was the familiar consideration that expenditure cuts tend to hit particular identifiable interest groups, while tax increases can be spread more thinly across society, that ultimately became the deciding factor in shaping the January 1982 Budget—a budget which proposed the largest increase ever in taxation in the history of the state. Though it was never implemented in full, this budget marked a turning-point in that, even when watered down by the new Government in March 1982, it effectively halted the spiral in the rate of public borrowing.

Moving ahead to 1984, we find that other considerations had begun to come to the fore. The policy of much higher taxation had been implemented; but, because of the escal-ator-like effect of debt interest, the additional taxation was sufficient only to prevent the current budget deficit from rising. It had been recognised that the scale of correction adopted would be sufficient to eliminate the deficit quickly only if inflation and interest rates fell sharply. But, though inflation did fall, real interest rates worldwide rose to record

levels, an unfortunate setback whose central role in perpetu-
ating the budgetary crisis has not always been recognised.
The process of identifying wasteful government expenditure
programmes was not yet bearing the hoped-for fruits. But
above all unemployment had virtually doubled in three
years, and the economy was in a bad slump (despite the
somewhat misleading statistics for manufacturing growth).
Hitherto neglected ideas now began to receive more attention: the oversimplified doctrines of the earlier years needed
revision.

Three partly incompatible ideas became important. First,
there was the idea that taxation did matter and that the
increase in taxation had significantly contributed to the
slump. This was a widely held opinion and by no means
confined to those on the right of centre. Second, some said
that a restrictive fiscal stance was doomed to fail: that it
would inevitably lead to a downward spiral of deepening
recession and widening deficits. Members of the trade union
movement were the most vocal supporters of this viewpoint.
A third, and more complex, view may have underlain the
widely read report on Employment and Unemployment
prepared by the Economic and Social Research Institute. It is
hard to determine precisely what its position was, but it
seemed to imply that while fiscal correction was necessary,
— and the sooner the better — the process would seriously
weaken the private sector of the economy. Accordingly the
public sector must itself generate economic activity both in
the commercial field and in further expansion of state
services. This activity would require lower pay levels in the
public service and a further increase in taxation.

I think that each of these ideas had some impact on the
evolution of government policy in 1984-7, and in particular
on the policies announced in the National Plan *Building on
Reality*. The first idea had its counterpart in the ceiling
which that plan proposed for the share of taxation in

GNP—though it would have been better if this had been supplemented with action on removing the worst distortions of the tax code itself. The second idea, though never accepted in government circles, had a pale reflection in the very limited degree of fiscal retrenchment pursued after 1984. Proponents of the third idea would have welcomed the large-scale public employment schemes of the Plan.

Preparing the Plans

A Plan had also been published by the Fianna Fáil Government in 1982, shortly before the November General Election of that year. In both cases, but especially with the 1984 Plan *Building on Reality*, the emphasis had changed, by comparison with the Plans of previous decades, to planning the State's finances rather than the private economy. This reflected both the policy preoccupations of the day and the shift in thinking that had occurred since the early 1970s regarding the ability of government planning documents to provide a useful input into sectoral economic planning.

The contrasting approaches adopted by the two Governments in consulting experts in drawing up their plans provide an insight into the administrative system as well as into the contrasts between the *modus operandi* of the political parties. To guide them in preparing the 1984 Plan, the Coalition Government adopted the original approach of appointing a National Planning Board formed of seven persons who were not civil servants. This approach contrasted with that taken by the Fianna Fáil Government of 1982 who had established an *ad hoc* steering group, composed of top civil servants (at the level of Departmental Secretary) together with the Director of the Economic and Social Research Institute and the Deputy General Manager of the Central Bank, to put together drafts of the 1982 Plan *The Way Forward*. The 1982 Steering Group was thus

15

composed of 'insiders'; the 1983-84 Planning Board of 'outsiders'.

This insider-outsider distinction had several consequences. For instance, the Steering Group did not address themselves directly to the public, but contributed to the formulation of the 1982 Plan in the normal manner of confidential advisers; in contrast, the Planning Board published a major and unexpurgated report containing its own recommendations and prognosis.

The members of the Steering Group could call upon the resources of their Departments to flesh out their ideas: since these persons would subsequently be carrying out the policies, the danger of official resistance to implementation was small. On the other hand, the Steering Group approach could not be expected to, and did not, produce a radically different set of policies to those already espoused by Departments.

When the Planning Board was established within months of the publication of *The Way Forward* it was inevitable that, being outsiders, its members would arrive at different conclusions to the Steering Group, and this meant that the Board was hardly likely to be welcomed by the insiders. It should come as no surprise, then, that the Board was not encouraged, by senior civil servants, to become actively involved in day-to-day policy; and although it called upon Departmental sources for factual material, the Board was not privy in any detail to the business of Government. This isolation greatly reduced the potential contribution of the Planning Board in 1983-84.

While the 1982 (Fianna Fáil) Plan still adhered to the objective of eliminating the current budget deficit by 1987, it envisaged very substantial borrowing for capital purposes. The Planning Board's 1984 approach was quite different. Since all of the interest on the greatly increased National Debt, as well as the extra burden of unemployment payments, added to current expenditure, it would be impossible to eliminate the budget deficit in any reasonable timescale, so they sought an alternative benchmark. The new objective which they espoused also involved eliminating a current deficit, but now the deficit was adjusted for cyclical factors such as high unemployment. The Board concluded that eliminating this cyclically adjusted deficit would involve a current budget deficit of some five per cent of GNP by 1987. This was certainly a much more realistic objective and the very independence of the National Planning Board gave it a credibility which an 'inside' document might not have secured. Henceforth any attempt by the Government to aim for a tougher objective would appear doctrinaire. Nevertheless, the Board's analysis came in for much criticism as being too soft and in particular as involving a level of borrowing which could prove unsustainable. The Central Bank rejected the target as inadequate, and there were doubts about the calculations which converted the concept of a cyclical adjustment to the target of five per cent.

The National Planning Board's report *Proposals for Plan* was not seen as itself being the Plan; but why a further document was needed is an interesting question in itself. After all, it would have been possible for the Government simply to announce that it had adopted the report in its entirety or in part and then act accordingly. I am not quite sure of all the considerations which led to the preparation of a further document. Some of these considerations will emerge in later sections below; in the context of this section one can remark that *Proposals for Plan* did not explicitly specify the balance between expenditure cuts and tax increases. Secondly, it did not provide a clear target for the overall borrowing requirement. Finally, the report posed a challenge for Government in projecting a massive increase in unemployment (of 50,000 persons in three years) over the period of the Plan.

17

Nevertheless, the Board had pointed clearly to the need to restrain tax increases, even going so far as to suggest that to employ an additional public servant would, because of the extra tax needed to finance this expenditure, result in lower employment overall. Of course there was also popular dissatisfaction with the rapid increase in the tax burden, so the Government may not have needed this theoretical argument to guide it in its strategic decision to place a ceiling on taxation for subsequent years at its 1984 level. This proved to be the most firm benchmark of the 1984 Plan, as it was more or less adhered to in the budgets of 1985 and '86.

The Target for Borrowing

On the question of overall borrowing, the Government was not in a position to be as vague as the Planning Board. The Board had eschewed the idea of a fixed budget for capital spending, saying simply that the volume of such spending should depend upon the availability of worthwhile and remunerative projects. But the Board's view in this regard did not in my view take adequate account of the need to signal clearly to sceptical financial markets that the Government would be relying less and less on borrowing. In order to convince the financial markets that policy was now on a sustainable course, there had to be a ceiling on borrowing too.

The precise borrowing ceiling was decided by the Government early on in the process of drawing up *Building on Reality* in May 1984. They were presented with a number of scenarios each involving a different level of borrowing, with estimated implications for employment, growth, the balance of payments and the National Debt. The chosen ceiling reflected a compromise between the need to protect employment and living standards in the short run and the need to present a credible borrowing profile to the financial markets. It represented the highest level of borrowing consistent with stabilising National Debt (as a proportion of GNP) within the life of the Government. Even with the benefit of hindsight it seems hard, on a balanced view, to fault the target as such. Certainly, no higher level of borrowing could have been rigorously defended as representing sustainable policy. Some thought the target was too weak: the Central Bank expressed this view in public. But it was also the strictest target that politicians could see their way to achieving: had there been a way of making a weaker target credible, they would have opted for it.

The failure to keep to this borrowing ceiling[1] is not part of our story here: the deviations were not strategic but reactive. It is too early to say definitively why the economy underperformed even relative to what were regarded as gloomy predictions in the Plan. The conventional wisdom is that more reliance on expenditure cuts and a better structure of taxation and social welfare would have helped. It is to these issues, and how policy in relation to them was formed, that we turn next.

WHAT

Cutting Public Spending

A ceiling on both taxation and borrowing implies a ceiling on spending: the ceiling that came out of the 1984 planning exercise was a good deal lower than the spending that would naturally emerge from existing spending programmes. This should have sent government advisers back to first principles in attempting to suggest an approach to spending restraint, and to some extent it did so.

What should the government spend money on? This is obviously a crucial question where financial stringency prevails. In the world in which we live it is rarely asked in this form, however, but in its imperfect converse: what should the government stop spending money on? The difference is

19

crucial. Comparisons with other wealthier countries immediately suggest a review of those public spending projects which might be undertaken in Ireland, and which fall naturally to the public rather than the private sector. Many of these fine airport improvements, rapid transit systems and local social services which we admire in other countries are appropriate only to a much higher level of national income. But there are spending opportunities which would outperform some of the programmes on which public money has been and is being spent. One of the most debilitating aspects of the policy environment in the past few years has been the practical necessity to identify and cut out inferior or plain wasteful spending programmes before one can even think about new spending plans. Inevitably long-term positive planning suffers under such circumstances.

Several points arise concerning the formulation of policy. Firstly, there is the momentum of existing programmes, partly reflecting political pressures, partly contrived by the initiators of the programmes who insert the thin end of a wedge-shaped programme whose size in later years has a natural growth pattern. Secondly, the fact that most public servants have been nurtured in a culture where value for money is not a prime consideration has resulted in a situation where, on the whole, the permanent administration has not only failed to guide and encourage government in the thankless task of cutting back, but has been apparently unable to develop policy of the type which does not impose a burden on the taxpayer. (The Department of Finance is not part of this culture but its role is seen as one-sided by spending departments and politicians alike). Thirdly, there has been a failure at the political level to use political criteria to replan and redirect Government spending to an extent that would both meet the need for an overall reduction and also allow worthwhile expansion in hitherto negelected areas.

The Cash Limit Approach

The National Planning Board addressed the question of what spending cuts ought to be made. Though carefully argued, their answer was not a satisfactory one for Government to adopt. Apart from a small number of specific cuts which they advocated, the bulk of the needed cutbacks were to be achieved by a uniform reduction in the cash allocations to each spending programme. No doubt the Board felt that there was insufficient detailed knowledge about the programmes to allow them to establish exactly what should be cut. There are some theoretical advantages in the idea of central administration setting a cash limit for specific programmes, allowing each programme manager to use local knowledge to best operate the programme within the given limits. But these advantages will only be realised if the cash limit is binding and seen to be so. Otherwise programme managers who have objectives which do not coincide with that of government will devote their efforts to generating the maximum pressure to get what they want. They can do this in a variety of ways, for example cutting out the most valuable parts of the programme first so as to create a public outcry. Or they can spend at an excessive level up until the last few weeks of the year, thereby contriving a cash crisis. Thus cash limits can perversely induce the exact opposite to the intended effect: bad management rather than good.

Cash limits applied through a uniform reduction of all programmes are unlikely to result in the equal sharing of the burden which presumably underlies this kind of approach. Many state programmes have an underlying momentum in their overall cost. The numbers in education, for instance, will continue to grow for demographic reasons for some years to come. Likewise, the number of beneficiaries of social welfare shows no signs of diminishing, rather the contrary. Training programmes are at present heavily funded by

21

the EEC. If that funding is cut back, then those programmes will also have to be curtailed unless they too are to generate a rapid increase in costs to the taxpayer. Apart from the large telecommunications and electricity investment schemes of the 1970s, few spending programmes lessen over time. The greater the growth momentum of a particular programme, the greater the likely cost of a particular percentage cut in its funding. The uniform reduction approach is too crude an instrument and could only be defended on the grounds that government is either unwilling or unable to decide upon priorities and keep to its decision.

The Role of Decentralised Management

Perhaps then government should devote its attention to seeking out the real inefficiencies in public spending? I doubt it. Of course there is waste in public spending programmes in the sense that the objectives of the programmes could be achieved at lower resource cost: but it is a task for managers of the programmes to identify cost savings which still allow the achievement of objectives. The government has its part to play in that process. It must create the conditions without which managers cannot be expected to perform well. Such conditions are usually taken to mean an adequate remuneration package, but in my view it is far more important that programme managers are given clear objectives, so that they know when they are getting results. While this principle is almost self-evident, it is rarely applied. In particular, managers are often confused as to whether and to what extent they should preserve employment when it entails increasing the cost of public services or imposing an additional burden on the taxpayer. Cost savings in the provision of public services almost always means a reduction in direct employment, at least when it is not possible to contemplate a big expansion in the volume supplied.

Time and again our intelligence is affronted by spurious

arguments designed to obstruct the efficient provision of public services, or even, as when the obsolescent Whitegate oil refinery was bought by the State, to increase the cost of existing goods, in this case petroleum products. A related example is the state-owned factory, now closed, which for years produced a petrol additive which Whitegate was obliged to use even though it added to the cost of petrol to the motorist—and reduced the excise revenue—without adding to its quality. The net social cost of this factory, which employed about two dozen workers, was in the region of one million pounds a year, but it was—for a long time—nobody's job to avoid this cost, concealed as it was in a fraction of a penny per litre.

It is not always jobs that are at stake: should the ESB be pressed to burn gas when oil is available more cheaply? Of course not; nothing could be more demoralising to a management bent on achieving cost effectiveness. The only reason such a course could seem attractive was that it generated an immediate revenue flow to Bord Gais Éireann (and thus to the Exchequer).

In order to eliminate waste, then, the government's job must be to establish the structures and the guidelines under which delegated management can perform, and then to respect those structures. This kind of mundane structure-building does not come naturally to politicians; the time-scale for results is long relative to the electoral cycle. *Therefore it should be to the foreground in the hidden agenda of the permanent civil service.* Curiously there is a line of opposition to this reasoning, one version of which runs as follows. 'If we encourage governments to establish clear objectives for state-sponsored companies (as advocated by the National Planning Board, and incorporated in *Building on Reality*, but not yet implemented) it will not be long before each company will be whinging for subventions to cover social services not explicitly provided for in the

23

statement of objectives.' While such thinking is all too pervasive in Irish public life, I am not sure that there is no basis for it. But it betrays a lack of confidence that is ultimately devastating to good policy; not confidence in the abstract, but confidence in people—the confidence of public servants in each other's judgment and motivation, and in the government's commitment and ability to brush aside short-term pressures.

The Role of Political Decisions

It is, however, an illusion that the elimination of waste, as I have defined it, will be enough to resolve the government's budgetary problems. The savings from elimination of waste are especially valuable because they do not simply transfer a burden from the public Exchequer to private households, but experience in other countries suggests that the speed with which such savings can be achieved is not great. Furthermore, the bulk of public spending is in the areas of income maintenance, and in health and education services which, in large part, substitute for private provision of the same services. But how, then, is government to decide where the axe is to fall? It has to be recognised that, while it has important technical aspects, this sort of decision is essentially political, not technical. There is absolutely no point in deciding that public spending must be cut back without simultaneously facing up to the reality that this process will involve imposing heavy losses on some people. Different approaches to the cutbacks will imply different losers.

Well-designed spending cuts can also yield efficiency gains: if patients have to pay for hospital services, then doctors will be slower to require use of these expensive facilities; if cuts in social welfare payments are concentrated on reducing the high rates of payment to those who are most likely to find other job opportunities, then the labour market

24

is likely to function more effectively. But the relative technical or efficiency advantages of different areas of cutback are not as large as their relative distributional impacts. When government really decides where the axe is to fall it will do so on political and not on technical criteria.

Only a firm political commitment will make cuts stick when the most modest cutback results in intensive lobbying. Within four months of the publication of *Building on Reality* the Government had capitulated on the main cutback foreshadowed in that document: the cash limit on the public service pay bill. It did not have the necessary political commitment to that policy, so it could be side-tracked by considerations such as the fear of public service strikes, and the claimed advantages of adherence to the established arbitration procedure, all of which were known before *Building on Reality* was published. Some members of the Government may feel that publication of the cash limit was only a bargaining ploy: as such it could only have undermined the Government's credibility and fuelled public cynicism.

The Role of the Civil Service

But it would help if there was an administrative back-up which could flesh out proposals for cuts where their adoption is envisaged by government. Because the spending Departments often feel that their function is to point out the needs of their client group and the advantages reaped from spending in their area, this cannot always be left to the Departments concerned. A standard mechanism for getting around this difficulty is the establishment of an *interdepartmental committee*. At its best, the interdepartmental committee is a powerful instrument of policy. In the context of spending cuts it will combine the financially conservative influence of the Department of Finance (which is almost always represented), with the detailed know-how of the spending departments and the political sensitivity of a ministerial adviser or of the Taoiseach's Department. Contrary to popular opinion, there are many able and experienced civil servants who can be called on to act on such committees. They will have a good knowledge of existing programmes here and often an awareness of recent experiments in Britain and elsewhere. (Unfortunately, before a new idea can receive the blessing of the Irish civil service, it must still usually have been adopted earlier in Britain. Not a few schemes have been copied here just as their weaknesses were becoming evident across the Irish Sea.) The ideal committee member will combine loyalty to her minister and department (by faithfully expressing their views and apprehensions), with an intellectual integrity which forces her to consider each question on its merits.

Needless to say, not all interdepartmental committees work so smoothly. In some cases members are given such restrictive marching orders by their superiors, or their ministers, that no progress can be made. Policy design needs a factual base and the facts may be fully available only to the spending department. It is easy for that department to prevent the relevant information from emerging. Lying, or a refusal to provide requested information is not necessary: to know precisely what information to ask for often requires specialist knowledge; the well-posed question is its own answer.

Another difficulty is that many civil servants have been brought up in a tradition where it is difficult for them to think independently. The expressed view of their minister is for them the last word, and should not be disputed. I was once taken aback when a senior and otherwise able official withdrew from a particular committee of which I was also a member, sending a substitute apparently because I had made some harsh criticisms of a recently published White Paper prepared in his Department; it was not that he had been involved in its preparation, but apparently that he could not function in an environment where recently enunciated government policy was being openly questioned.

If there is a gap, it is most often in the broader vision; a view of the overall economic impact of proposals, or the long-term impact on social structures. There are several reasons why this gap may have emerged, but one relates to the administrative structure itself. In this small country the number of experts with the kind of breadth of vision which is required for designing major policy initiatives will always be small, and the permanent administration will only attract a proportion of these. The administration is divided into so many little boxes that there are not enough able people to go around. The interdepartmental committee is only a partial solution in this context, and a floating 'think tank' would also be of limited use, because of its inevitable lack of integration into the real administrative structure (compare the experience of the National Planning Board).

In particular there are too many autonomous government departments; several mergers, effectively restoring the position of the 1950s, would result in a better use of the available administrative resources. Important planning initiatives could then be developed within the resulting larger departments, without the need for interdepartmental leavening to achieve the necessary mixture of objectivity, experience and ability. It may be added that a larger department would have the resources to deal more effectively also with sudden crises that can at present expose experience and ability deficiencies in a smaller department especially if, though out of its depth, it protects its autonomy by attempting to cope with the crisis on its own. Of course if there must be fifteen ministers, my proposal would not leave enough Departments to go around, but that would hardly be a sufficient objection.

Ministerial Advisers

What about ministerial advisers? This term (variously rendered in official documents as 'Economic Adviser', 'Special Adviser' or 'Special Assistant') covers a number of entirely different kinds of function. At one extreme, some advisers are employed primarily to maintain a liaison with party activists and members of the Oireachtas. They act as the political eyes and ears of the minister, and may also be involved in speech-writing of the narrowly political kind which permanent civil servants are not expected to provide. At the opposite extreme, others are selected to strengthen the professional resources available to ministers and government; these need not be party activists, though journalists always assume they are. A few versatile souls combine attributes of both species. The then Secretary of the Department of the Public Service was not incorrect when he wrote recently that an objective of the appointment of advisers 'is to give ministers an alternative to official advice from people who share the government's aims and philosophy.'[2] But his description wrongly suggests a monolithic civil service and an exclusively confrontational role for the adviser *vis-à-vis* the permanent officials. An important part of the adviser's function is to be a conduit of information and opinions from many sources. It is often forgotten that decisions of any significance are taken at cabinet and collectively. Ministers need to have recourse to something other than the often turgid, and sometimes cryptically drafted, government memoranda covering other ministers' proposals if they are to make a contribution to discussion in cabinet.

The function of each minister's departmental officials will primarily be to comment on the proposals only in so far as they directly concern the department. The adviser, on the other hand, will make it his business to inform himself of the background to proposals; he will ascertain why alternatives

28

which have been suggested elsewhere—by academics or other commentators—are not part of the official proposal, and he will weigh the practical and administrative objections which are being advanced against these alternatives. He will function most effectively where he has been able to establish a relationship of mutual trust with the permanent officials concerned. And the permanent official of another department who wishes to stress some aspect for the attention of a minister can do no better than obtain the ear of that minister's adviser. Some ministerial advisers have been drawn from among the permanent officials: it is not hard to find civil servants who share, at least in a general way, 'the government's aims and philosophy'. Nor are the expressed differences between the philosophies of the major parties so great as to preclude such a person from resuming his role as a loyal permanent official under a new government.

There are still permanent civil servants who look on all advisers with deep suspicion. Some, who have seen their proposals, which were perfectly coherent and sensible in the memorandum through which they were submitted, emerge from cabinet discussion distorted beyond recognition, blame the advisers. Government meetings are attended neither by advisers nor the permanent officials, but to the latter the adviser can seem part of the process which diminishes the chances of a preferred proposal being adopted as submitted.

Pressure Groups

A much more open process of government decision-making would reduce these conflicts between official and advisers' views to the extent that public debate would supersede them. But a more public decision process including, for example the publication of government memoranda, would carry the cost, in today's political environment, of strengthening the hand of special interest groups in opposing measures which might damage them.

Some commentators have been critical of the abrupt manner in which the few cutbacks that were adopted over the past few years were announced. It is undeniable that, in a perfect world, all interested parties would be consulted to ensure full availability of all relevant information. The reality is, however, that in most cases the views of the interested parties are well known, and that they are unlikely to contribute constructively in designing a measure that will damage them when experience suggests that lobbying for abandonment of the measure altogether stands a good chance of success. Ministers, too, agree to restrictive measures only with reluctance: who can blame those who implement the decisions for doing so in haste for fear that the ministers' courage will forsake them again?

FOR WHOM

The Tax Policy Deadlock

Problems of taxation and redistribution have loomed large in economic policy debate of the 1980s. It is not hard to see why: for taxation there was the increase of about one-third in the real burden of taxation between 1979 and 1984; about the same as the increase in the numbers in receipt of income maintenance payments from the State. Two full-scale Government Commissions have reported: one, on Taxation, in five volumes published between 1982 and 1986; the other, on Social Welfare, in a single volume, published in 1986. Yet, though many initiatives have been announced, and some implemented, during the past few years, there have been few really striking changes in the structure of taxation or of the other mechanisms of redistribution. Neither Commission's report has so far elicited a government policy paper.

How can we explain this lack of action? Does it reflect inertia or deadlock? It cannot be attributed to lack of public interest in the subject nor to a shortage of recommendations for change. Some of the blame might be laid on the fact that there were minority governments in 1981-82, and that the Coalition Government of 1982 to 1987 was composed of two parties who were likely to have fairly sharp differences of view on the questions involved. But this would be an over-simplification.

The Commission on Taxation

While everyone agrees that neither the tax nor the social welfare system is satisfactory, there is little agreement among the experts, whether economists, accountants, social workers or lawyers, on which reforms are the best. If politicians are deadlocked, this should not wholly mask the elements of intellectual deadlock which also exist. The situation may best be illustrated, perhaps, by the experience (to date) of the reports of the Commission on Taxation, though we will not here attempt a detailed account of the intellectual debate on tax reform.[3]

It is a commonplace, but we must not forget that most people's basic idea of tax reform is that taxes should be (a) lower, (b) effectively collected from those at present avoiding their fair share, and (c) levied mainly on those wealthier than oneself. While the question of lower taxation was not part of the Commission on Taxation's brief, they had many things to say about greater effectiveness of collection (though they did not of course fall into the trap of assuming the existence of a shadowy plutocrat class who could easily bear most of the burden of tax if only they could be tracked down). But the main contribution of the Commission was a much more subtle one, and not one that was directed to any of the most common demands of tax reform as caricatured above. The Commission's innovation was to seek efficiency of the structure and to provide a unifying principle which could guide Governments in designing tax changes.

The Commission on Taxation took it as axiomatic that, in most cases, high tax rates distort behaviour and lead to losses of economic efficiency. Different rates of tax levied on different but related activities result in avoidance techniques which are not only sources of inefficiency, but, when successful, result in a failure of the objectives of the difference in rates. Thus high marginal rates of tax on high incomes can easily be avoided, at least by the wealthiest income earners in society, and the differences between the rates of tax on different classes of company income have led to tax avoidance mechanisms of an extraordinary complexity, to the point where the abolition of some loopholes can result in the closure of substantial companies. It is impossible to summarise a thousand pages in one sentence, but, generally speaking, the Commission concluded that substantial advantages could be achieved by charging tax at a single rate, limiting exemptions from this tax to the minimum. This perspective guided not only their views on direct taxation, reported in 1982, but also their approach to indirect taxation as presented in their third report of 1984. (The Commission also proposed a direct progressive expenditure tax on higher income groups.)

An interesting dialectical process ensued. In the first phase discussion surrounding the Commission's report became polarised between those who foresaw gains from a lowering of the high marginal tax rates which they were paying, and an opposing group who feared considerable losses for lower income groups resulting from the abolition of personal allowances. Soon, however, the upper middle-class support wavered as interest rates soared during 1982, and the beneficiaries of mortgage interest relief saw that they too might suffer from the proposed reform of direct taxation. The issue of efficiency was not to the foreground of this discussion. It seems that the Commission left themselves open to attack from all quarters on distributional questions because they presented only a structural framework, not detailed calculations with specific rates of tax showing gainers and losers. This was also complicated by the brushing under the carpet of the problems of needy losers who were to be catered for through unspecified changes in the Social Welfare system. Presumably the Commission did not regard the redistributional potential of the tax system as its most important feature (many studies have stressed that the tax system plays a comparatively minor role by comparison with expenditure measures, as things stand in redistributing income). However, this neglect has seriously impeded acceptance of their proposals, in that it is precisely the short-term redistribution effect that receives most attention by Government in considering taxation reform.

One might suppose that the permanent civil service could have provided a counterweight to the short-term preoccupations of politicians in this matter, and indeed it did have other concerns, but they did not support the recommendations of the Commission either. Senior officials took pains to express their doubts publicly.[4] Apart from questions of redistribution, their main fear was that the revenue generated by the Commission's proposals would be insufficient by comparison with the yield of the existing tax regime, and that a serious fiscal crunch would follow any attempt to implement the report. This fear was probably felt on more than one plane: there were specific disputes, notably over the likely yield of a modified corporation tax; but there must also have been a more deepseated unease. Consider how easy it is to abolish an unpopular tax (like domestic rates) and how hard to introduce an alternative that really generates revenue (especially if the main appeal of the new tax is that it is more conducive to economic efficiency, as with taxation at source of deposit interest). Surely part of the official opposition to the main thrust of the

Commission's first report was that a government that embarked on implementing the report might easily end up adopting only the most palatable parts of the package. But by adopting this view, the officials effectively acquiesced in an unsatisfactory and unsustainable tax system, closed the door on systematic reform and unwittingly encouraged more piecemeal tinkering with the tax code by politicians desperately seeking a way of reducing the unpopularity of taxation.

Only a minority of theoreticians remained who were attracted to the Commission's report, and their views were easily swept aside. The publication of a National Plan would have been a suitable opportunity to inaugurate the process of tax reform, but with administrative as well as political opposition swamping the theoretical arguments, it was perhaps inevitable that the Government all but buried the proposals in a handful of dismissive but superficial paragraphs of *Building on Reality*—though the drafting did allow a chink of hope for the future, and the Taoiseach himself stressed that reform was not ruled out, only postponed. Nevertheless, the popular reaction to the absence of any tax reform measures in the Plan was unfavourable, and within months a few of the Commission's ideas could be detected, though in a very muted form, in the tax measures of the 1985 Budget.

Even more serious in my view than the loss of the specific proposals of the Commission was the policy vacuum which was created by the Government's refusal to accept the unifying principle which the Commission had proposed. Into this vacuum rushed many diverse and mutually contradictory ideas, some for new *ad hoc* taxes, such as the 1986 levy on insurance companies; some for special tax reliefs, such as those for stock options, also in 1986. It is impossible to formulate tax policy in the absence of a guiding principle, because of the contradictions to which different approaches almost inevitably lead. Each of the measures introduced over the years, whether reliefs or impositions, has had something to recommend it; taken together they have created an un-attractive patchwork which is still receiving the attention of the seamstress.

The Commission on Social Welfare

There are some parallels and many contrasts in the case of the Commission on Social Welfare. Of course the latter did not follow the lead of the Taxation Commission, in estab-lishing a powerful analytical underpinning for its work;[5] accordingly most attention was focused on its specific recommendations. Once again opinion was polarised between winners and losers: in this case the winners were immediately identifiable among those dependent on social welfare payments on a long-term basis. They would, over a period of time, receive substantial real increases in the level of their income. As long-term beneficiaries had experienced real increases of up to 20 per cent during the 1980s already, this proposal was essentially a continuation of existing bipartisan policy. As such it was castigated by those who had criticised the steady growth in public spending generally. The proposals found little favour with the upper middle class who identified that policy as a contributory factor in increasing their tax bills.

If the Commission on Taxation neglected distributional implications, the Commission on Social Welfare, reporting four years after the first taxation report, and in a climate less hospitable to calls for redistribution, neglected the pressing demands of the Government's budget constraint, and the political resistance to tax increases.

At the time of writing neither Commission seems likely to have its recommendations implemented in full in any short timescale.[6] The policy deadlock has been worsened by the fact that the two reports are widely seen to have been at cross-purposes, the balance of priorities held by the members of the two Commissions having been quite different. Above all, although they remained in the public eye during the 1987 election campaign, neither Commission has apparently had a real political champion in government. Of the two, it is clearly the tax report which has the longer shelf-life. It may not be unrealistic to hope that the deplorable state of the tax code will sooner or later attract the attention of a secure government that is prepared to take the risks of a thoroughgoing reform.

HOW

Structures for Policy

The 1980s have seen as much as any previous decade of considered and published advice on *how* the economy and economic policy should be arranged. As well as the reports of the two major Commissions and of the National Planning Board, the intensive studies of the National Economic and Social Council into industrial policy may also be singled out. Yet little has been changed. It almost seems that, as the policy problems have grown, the average size of the policy steps actually taken has shrunk.

Some may argue that the recommendations were not good, or that the way our economy is organised does not require fundamental change. But I think that the widely felt malaise in society, traceable to economic underperformance, suggests that the political and administrative system has been successful neither in focusing on the major strategic issues facing the nation nor in formulating and carrying through coherent policy measures. An analysis of why this is so is beyond the scope of this paper. But I would like to select three features of the existing regimen which, however naïvely, it seems to me could easily be changed, and probably have been serious impediments to good policy; first, the obsessive secrecy surrounding all government business; second, the lack of authority of civil servants; and third, the universal attempt to achieve consensus.

Openness

We have already touched on the question of secrecy and it has many aspects. I accept that there are occasions when one would not wish to abandon secrecy. For instance, one may wish to preserve confidentiality if the privacy of an individual or the commercial interests of an enterprise are involved, because the organisation of our society appears to depend on the ability of individuals and firms to maintain confidentiality and because government will not be able to function credibly if it cannot offer confidentiality. But in practice, and in a small country, there is a tendency for government to indulge in far too many bilateral transactions with individuals and firms. It is probably simplistic to assert that the success of the British parliamentary and governmental tradition, on which the Irish system has been based, has relied on the notion that government must deal at arm's length with individuals and firms: rules that apply to one should apply to all. This tradition is not always adhered to in Britain, but it is rarely even acknowledged in Ireland. I can see no good coming out of the practice of individuals or firms lobbying ministers in secret: therefore the preservation of privacy need rarely dictate secrecy in government business.

The main pressure for maintaining secrecy comes from the desire of government to pretend that its policy is so self-evidently correct that there could have been no debate or disagreement about it, either among government ministers or their official advisers. This fiction is so far-fetched that it is hard to understand why anyone of intelligence should submit themselves to the inevitable ridicule which attends those who defend it in public. Yet it is the conventional understanding of the doctrine of collective responsibility of government ministers, enshrined in the Constitution. Unless they feel so strongly about a matter that they wish to resign from government, otherwise honest politicians pretend that they agree with measures which they actually find abhorrent. Such behaviour may not always be fully transparent to the public, but it damages the credibility of politicians, and causes them to be held in lower esteem. We have already mentioned the enthusiasm with which the press seizes on evidence of differences between ministers: but the novelty of such stories would rapidly fade if those ministers felt free to carry on policy debate more openly.

The gain from such openness could be enormous. Most policy discussions involve complexities of detail not apparent to the outside observer. I have rarely encountered an economic policy problem where the textbook model fitted the facts exactly. Each case has its own special features which may, or may not, be sufficiently important to dictate a departure from the conventional prescription. These special features are often the most colourful part of the description of the problem as presented to ministers and will accordingly dominate their consideration of it to the exclusion of general principles. Public debate of the issues is often carried out in ignorance of these special features, allowing ministers whose decisions are criticised to take comfort in the knowledge that the critique has not taken account of the special features which were decisive. But should they have been decisive? The absence of a comprehensive public debate prevents us from knowing for sure. The mechanics of decision-making behind closed doors are not themselves conducive to adequate decision-making.

We should bear in mind the circumstances and physical environment in which government deliberations are conducted. Fifteen ministers sit around an oval table which, more often than not, is covered with piles of memoranda, notes and coffee cups. The discussion will be conducted without the benefit of expert contributions from officials expert in the field under consideration. (Occasionally a senior civil servant may be called in to explain a technical point, but that is not the normal procedure.) The Secretary to the Government is present, but he is not seen as having a steering role at government meetings. The issue under consideration has been summarised in an often lengthy memorandum which has been prepared by the relevant department. This memorandum generally concludes with a jumble of critical comments from other departments, each with a rejoinder by the initiating department. Sometimes the memorandum is deliberately cryptic: a formal request, prepared by civil servants with an eye to the archives, for government approval *not* to go ahead with, say, a hospital extension or an RTC in Ballylobby may (especially if the memorandum includes an account of the strong desire of the Ballylobby community to see the project go ahead) conceal an expectation that the government will reject the ostensible request and order that building be commenced. No doubt, busy ministers often choose to bypass prolix or encoded documents and wait for their colleague's word of mouth presentation which can be expected to be more readily assimilated. Under these circumstances the final decision rests too heavily on the presentational and debating skills of individual ministers. The relative importance of technical factors may be overestimated or underestimated. Short-term political considerations will tend to receive too much weight, because each person contributing to the discussion in the room is accustomed to attaching weight to that kind of consideration.

This seems to be a silly way of reaching good decisions on complex issues. Instead I believe that publication of government memoranda should be the norm. This would allow the public debate to be conducted on the basis of common information. The political decisions could then be taken on the true political issues, and we would be spared the sight of ministers trying to justify their political actions by reference to technical arguments on which they are not competent to adjudicate. There would, of course, be cases where it would not be realistic to release the relevant documentation; but these would be the exception rather than the rule.

Some ministers have tended to leak documents selectively as a means of bringing public pressure to bear on some matter under government consideration: this gives us the worst of both worlds, as the selectivity in leaking distorts information. But leaking ministers have surely had the correct approach to collective responsibility. In a sensible interpretation, can collective responsibility mean much more than a responsibility not to undermine what has collectively been decided? To register dissent is not to undermine. Ministers should be free to argue their individual points of view openly, and if this generates at first a boisterous press and opposition excitement, that can only be a transitional phenomenon, to be succeeded by a more mature public debate which can involve opposition politicians as well as interested parties. This is, after all, too small a country not to have the benefit of as wide a debate as possible.

Another benefit of open policy debate is that a clear distinction between lobbying and consultation will emerge. Only when it is carried out in secret does lobbying become objectionable; in public its transparency limits its ability to deceive. Genuine consultation will emerge naturally as part of the public debate.

Of course there will always be secret discussions, and secret documents. Individual ministers will not necessarily find it in their interest to publicise their disagreements. What I am asking for is a change of attitude; a review of the current blanket presumption that to communicate is to violate some high principle.

More Powers for the Civil Service

The notion that government memoranda should be published generates a strength of reaction among civil servants that outsiders would find hard to understand. This is because memoranda are prepared by civil servants many of whom regard themselves as having no public views: their position is the minister's position, for to express a contrary view is to undermine the minister. Even allowing the present situation where the minister is the sole arbiter of departmental actions (to the point where, for example, no civil servant can be held accountable for wasteful expenditure, if the expenditure was in line with government policy and within the sums voted by the Oireachtas), the position taken by some officials is unduly timid. Nevertheless it has to be conceded that a decisive improvement will not be achieved until the long awaited extension of considerably more autonomy to departmental secretaries is implemented. There has been some move in this direction with the proposed independence of 'Executive Offices'.

But these offices will not have a policy role. The ministers and secretaries who are reluctant to see a change in the present arrangements foresee many problems. Consider a hypothetical example where the minister would like a new road to be built through his constituency, whereas traffic flows dictate that other roads should be built first. At present the minister wins his road, because it is his prerogative as a policy decision. But if the minister loses his absolute supremacy, there will be a confrontation as the secretary's job will be to avoid wasteful public expenditure. It is because neither ministers nor secretaries want this kind of potential for uncomfortable conflict that progress towards devolution has been slow. These are not good arguments against change.

Greater power must carry with it an appropriate accountability. Recently others[7] have begun to propose more radical constitutional reforms which would recast the role of ministers and departmental chief executives, giving the latter much more sweeping powers than elected representatives. Perhaps that is the way to go. But there is much that may be entrusted to civil servants even under the existing constitution. This is not the place to propose a detailed blueprint for the delegation of authority to civil servants, nor would I be qualified to do so. We have already, however, identified some of the inherent strengths of non-elected officials—their longer time horizons, their relative freedom from the pressures exerted by interest groups, their ability to cope with technical issues through efficient management of their resources of expert staff. It is the authority to exploit these strengths that must be given to them.

Civil servants with enhanced authority must also, of course, enter into the public policy debate. It is hard to see how a democracy can be effective otherwise. Having civil servants speak out on policy issues will not be the end of the world for ministers. The Central Bank has managed to do this for over thirty years without unduly hampering the independence of politicians.

What Should Politicians Do?

What would be left for politicians if policy debate were to be carried out in public and the civil servants given increased powers? The answer must be that politicians would take the final decisions; they would make political choices. Much too much energy is absorbed by politicians seeking consensus solutions, or what is known to economists as Pareto improvements: a Pareto improvement in society is achieved when *everyone* is made better off. The potential for Pareto improvements is small. Nearly every policy measure, however admirable, damages somebody. It is far more

42

fruitful to make progress in selected areas, forming coalitions who will accept packages, not all of which will be attractive to each, but which taken together, will offer the greatest long-term prospects for the greatest number. Unless no policy is good policy—a possibility which cannot be rejected out of hand—such log rolling must form the greater part of political compromise.

The relative absence of an ideological basis for the main political parties in Ireland is well-known. As a result most political disagreements focus on the interest groups who will gain or lose. But there are radically different views in Irish society as to how the economy can best be organised. The alignment of political parties with one or other of these views would help to enhance the quality of policy debate. Policy choices would be more decisive, perhaps reforming whole sections of economic organisation, where one view gained the upper hand. The tentative nature of the con-sensus-seeking policy-making style which we have experienced has allowed the economy to drift aimlessly, burdened ever more heavily by the cost and distortions of in-appropriate public spending, and indeed vulnerable too to the depredations of cartels, restrictive practices and powerful special interests that are somehow still tolerated.

So far, the eighties have seen no vintage years for innovative economic policy. Hamstrung first by world recession and then by a growing realisation of the immensity of the debt millstone, successive governments rejected each proposal for radical reorientation. Only with growing prosperity could any of the proposals be greeted with something approaching a consensus. Without consensus none seemed politically possible.

Yet without radical choices there is no prospect of the country breaking out of depression. Nevertheless we can take heart from the thought, increasingly evident from the result of four general elections, that timidity or inaction are not politically rewarded either. If this lesson is learnt and applied to the systematic implementation of considered reform, then there can be hope.

2. The Future of Education–Innovation, Continuation and Harnessing Technology

WHEN the European Institute of Education was set up in Paris in 1975 its first brochure stated that every European problem had an educational dimension and that every educational problem had a European dimension. The statement remains as true as it was then, although Europe itself has changed substantially in structure and mood over the years and educational issues and structures have changed perhaps even more. Within most nation states belonging to the Community there is still far too little basic education related to the making of Europeans. Although there have been encouraging developments in higher education, particularly in the ERASMUS scheme, which opens up fascinating new possibilities for student mobility, there remain formidable obstacles to European understanding within both national educational and communications systems.

There is another problem also. In recent years several European countries have proceeded to envisage or even to carry out educational reforms, sometimes but not always after an adequate domestic debate, without necessarily considering the directly relevant experience of other countries. Educational developments have taken place at best in parallel, at worst in opposition. Nor is it any consolation that since the Treaty of Rome virtually left out education altogether, there is no legal obligation to focus attention on why things should be otherwise. Failures to learn from each other are certainly not the fault of the officers of the Community in Brussels. They, indeed, have led the way, and have encouraged the pooling of experience and the exchange of ideas in face of national compartmentalisation.

Compartmentalisation, however, is not simply an aspect of the making of diverse national education policies. It affects the way in which education is considered in relation to other public issues. Educational policies cannot be considered in isolation. It is an aspect, too, of separated research. The European Institute of Education in Paris sensibly decided in 1983 to include in its title 'social policy' as well as 'education', partly because it was difficult to separate questions of education from questions of employment and unemployment and partly because to an increasing extent European governments were transferring a substantial part of their financial resources from ministries of education to ministries concerned with manpower. The process continues, but, so far, few educational research organisations have considered aspects of this transfer of responsibilities in other than financial terms.

Even within the Institute a further aspect of educational policy making—how to cope with the complex relationship between national educational and communications systems—has been little studied. While it is generally recognised that newspaper and book, screen and blackboard, and video and computer together influence our perceptions of Europe and of the world sometimes in complementary, sometimes in adversary, fashion, their impact has usually been the subject of charge and counter-charge rather than of research or, for that matter, of argument and counter-argument. 'Media' and 'education' fall into separate pigeon-holes. What is certain is that many elements in the present communications pattern do not so much limit understanding of Europe or of the world as contribute to the increase of misunderstanding. Again, there is no consolation in the fact that the point holds equally for domestic social and economic issues as for the issues of contemporary Europe as identified in Brussels or Strasbourg.

As far as education itself is concerned, it is fortunately a subject that is alive in most countries, not least in political circles, and it is not surprising that during the last five years more attention has been paid in many European countries to school education than to higher education. This attention to 'the foundations' has concentrated both on performance and on institutional structures. The debate has ranged widely over many aspects of the subject, particularly parental choice, teaching methods, examinations and, in Britain, whether or not there should be a national core curriculum, something taken for granted in most European countries, and, if so, what its constituent elements should be. Little attention has been paid, however, to the claims of the European Baccalaureate, an examination which now has general European standing. It has established itself in practice as one of the most imaginative ventures of recent years.

Concentration on the foundations is useful and necessary and it can be stimulating. Yet an exclusive preoccupation with the foundations would be unbalanced, even dangerous. Foundations exist at all times to support other things. In our own late-twentieth-century societies, which rely on sophisticated science and technology, education is rightly being considered more widely than ever before as life-long education; a point which was not fully appreciated in the nineteenth century when the public provision of school education was concerned with teaching the rules of literacy and numeracy in a disciplined manner. School education is not enough. Education is a process in which one phase is related to another, and the relationship between the phases, and the share of resources devoted to each of them is as important as what happens within each phase. Individuals learn at different paces, and there are always 'late developers' who have 'missed out'. We appreciate now that such people require something more than 'remedial education'. Experience has to be made use of at every point. All discussion about education should start on the basis of the continuity of the process and the importance of its substance.

It is unfortunate, however, that at a time when the content and structures of higher education raise interesting and challenging long-term issues across national frontiers, there has been a narrowing of horizons. Because of limitations on financial resources and, more seriously, damaging cuts, individual institutions spend a great deal of time and energy on their own limited, short-term affairs. Moreover, financial restraints often have the further effect of imposing a purely accounting approach to educational problems and priorities. Important though careful costing is, it is a mistake, as Patrick Lynch has recognised, to confuse management with accounting. The most able university managers have recognised this too, knowing of course, that it remains difficult, if the circumstances are wrong, for even the most enlightened of managers to translate the language of constraint into the language of opportunity. There is as much, if not greater need for leadership to express itself in a period of contraction as in a period of expansion.

In both periods it should be recognised that it is not enough to offer single-subject higher education. It has its place—and in a period of unemployment it is now a popular place for students—yet it should not dictate the pattern of higher studies. The ideal, already started in the 1960s, a very different decade from our own, is to study related specialised subjects within shared contexts so that the benefits of specialised training are combined with the advantages of a more general education. There is no one single structure of higher education that achieves this ideal, but it remains an ideal whatever the circumstances. Even if school education were to become less specialised than it is, there would still be a need for interdisciplinary work in universities and in other institutions of higher education. It not only prepares people to cope with change and with uncertainty, but is a necessary foundation for problem-orientated research.

The problems that confront society do not usually fall neatly within the boundaries of academic disciplines: they require a convergence of disciplines, both in methods and in insights. No single academic specialism, least of all economics, is enough. In the future, as in the present, this will remain true in relation, for example, to the problems of the 'inner cities' or of 'race relations' or, indeed, of both taken together. During the 1960s there was too much emphasis on sociology without economics. Now the danger is too much economics with too little sociology. The kind of education we organise, both through teaching and research, should be directly related to wise policy making. The two topics may be separated in essays but they cannot be separated in life.

The full implications of treating education as a lifelong process have not as yet been fully appreciated, but there is now empirical evidence on which to frame educational policy-making. Of all the new educational institutions that were created during the 1960s it may well be that Britain's Open University most clearly pointed the way. The original idea behind it was a simple one—that of increasing access to higher education through the communications system, particularly television, which had burst its way into the home during the previous ten years. There was a convergence of technological change and social thinking, for the widening of access through the use of new technology was to make up the past deficiencies. University education, as generally understood, necessarily dealt in limited numbers, it seemed, and the social mix of undergratuates was biased. A 'University of the Air' would be available for all.

In retrospect, as at the time, the idea sounds exciting. In fact, however, experience changed it. Indeed, before the experience had begun to accumulate, the implications of the idea had already been pushed further by the Planning Committee. The communications system was not to be the only provider. Nor within it was television to be the only element. Radio came into its own. It was realised that the individual student would need access to books and access to people, and a correspondence system was devised in which the student's tutor, a familiar figure in some but by no means all traditional universities, was a key figure. In other words, the individual was to learn through a battery of methods, old and new, together designed to enable him to learn as independently as possible and at his own pace. The openness of social access was maintained—'first come, first served' was the only principle of admission—although 'foundation courses' (the term brings back the old metaphor) were devised to introduce to 'higher education' students who were unfamiliar not only with the content of different studies but with ways of learning. A more challenging metaphor would be 'gateway'. The challenge was particularly interesting in relation to mathematics, a necessary key to all work in science and technology and a valuable key to all work in the social sciences.

The record of what has happened since 1970 is encouraging, although the student population, a cross-section of the population, is more biased towards particular social groups and particular parts of the country than some of the idealists of the 1980s would have wished. Each year as many would-be students have to be turned away as are accepted. The annual output of graduates is over 20,000, which means that by the year 2000 Open University graduates will be able to exert a sizeable presence and influence in national life. The 100,000th graduation is expected, God willing, to take place in 1989 or 1990.

What is important in the historical record is that there has been adaptability as well as development from the first guiding principles. In a society which pays increasing attention to science and technology, the proportion of students studying these subjects has substantially increased, though they are encouraged to relate their science and technology to issues of social use as well as individual advancement. Thus, a tendency common to all universities in all parts of Europe is as apparent in the Open University as anywhere else, with the pressure coming from the demand side. Yet on the supply side there has been an equally significant sign of adaptability in the remarkable expansion of continuing education, education not leading up to degrees but directly related to social need. The whole idea of continuing education, a key idea, has been thought out afresh.

Higher education is less and less restricted to one age group. Nor is it thought of as requiring a degree or a diploma to be complete. Again, the lesson is not specific to the Open University or to one country. Given both social and demographic factors, all universities are being forced to rethink their role as multi-age institutions catering both for the first stages of higher education and later stages which will not be the same for different individuals. There is now very relevant experience of change in France, Germany and Holland, for example, and it is increasingly recognised that in the light of it we have to reconsider the role of education for the 16 to 21 year-old age group.

In the twenty-first century universities will also have to reconsider their role as local, national and international institutions, and in this connection also there have been interesting recent developments. It seems likely that there will be more 'networking' between universities, more common programming, hopefully far more mobility of students and staff. The expanded ERASMUS scheme has now received its first block of applications, a dauntingly large one, and it is clear that as the whole scale of the enterprise has changed there are entirely new perspectives. Meanwhile, as the COMETT training programme has established itself, obstacles to further progress can be identified; the first of its objects 'to give a European dimension to co-operation between universities and enterprises in training relating to innovation and the development and application of new technologies, and related social adjustment.' Promoting the right relationships between industry and institutions of higher education can still remain difficult, however, in this field.

How to relate innovation to tradition is a subject of continuing interest in higher education and the study of it demands a long time span. Because the horizons of educational policy making are always changing, those concerned with it, while being realistic about the present, cannot avoid long-term views. There is a commonplace difference in this respect between education and politics, although there is always a hope in society, realised only intermittently, that politicians, too, will/could, despite all the immediate pressures, show signs of being influenced by long-term vision.

They may not have fully appreciated yet that the university of the twenty-first century will be a different institution in many different ways from that of the traditional university. People will want to have access to it as a resource centre in society at different points in their lives and for different purposes, and they will be influenced by family circumstances as well as by ambition or the desire for personal enrichment. The university of the future is not likely to be a standardised institution, however, for there will be a need for resource centres of different kinds. Some will be very closely related to their local community; some genuinely international. There should be no talk of a common curriculum here or adaptability will be lost. Nor should trust be placed on one single way of learning. Above all, there should be freedom for experiment.

The experiment will have to take account of new patterns of communication, for the communications system continues to change in such a dramatic way that the term 'communications revolution', coined in the 1950s to describe the change, is now taken for granted. Recent advances in technology including computers, videos and satellites, have rendered obsolete much of the technology of the 1950s. Video makes possible an expansion of home learning at lower cost which was not clearly anticipated in 1970. There is a new convergence, therefore, with a social emphasis in this case not so much on widened access as on upgraded manpower. There is little sign that those in charge of the making of communication policies—the term itself is controversial—are any more aware of the complexities of changing structures than those who are in charge of the making of educational policies, but there is often more immediate political interest in 'information technology', a field now promoted in most countries, than there is in higher education. There are even signs of a backlash, particularly in Germany, against its influence on other and older aspects of higher education.

Within education itself technology should not be thought of as anything more than instrumental. Yet it is one of the purposes of education to undertake serious study of technologies in perspective and to stimulate interest in the possible alternative modes of their organisation and use. We have to make the future, not simply to adjust. This was a point emphasised in one of the most interesting early Open University courses on Society, Technology and Design. The introduction to a book of readings *Man-Made Futures* (1974), edited by Nigel Cross, David Elliott and Robin Roy, stated clearly that 'whereas once the direction of technological change seemed to be inevitable, or decided by private interests, there is now a growing belief that alternative directions can and should be the subject of open debate.'

That kind of debate requires convenient and acceptable centres, and universities, because of their critical role in society, are centres where it can and should be conducted. In the future as in the past, society will need something more than resource centres where needs are determined by governments. It will need centres of initiative where new ideas and undertakings can emerge. Some of these are bound to be critical of society as it is and as it has been. If universities did not exist they would have to be invented for this reason alone, though they might not be given the name or linked to a tradition which incorporates many other elements also. The sub-institution of the new University of Sussex which I am most proud to have founded is the Science Policy Research Unit, SPRU. Once founded, it had a life of its own.

Without looking as far as the twenty-first century, it is clear that the traditional pattern of 'higher education' as provided in universities and in other institutions of higher education cannot be taken for granted. Indeed, the pattern already varies in different countries—it began to diverge most sharply in the nineteenth century, and in most countries it already includes 'non-traditional' elements introduced during the last thirty years, the University of Sussex being the first of the new British universities of the 1960s, and the Open College, concerned explicitly with non-degree work in 'further education', being the most recent. Many of the recent developments, unlike the University of Sussex or the Open College, planned outside university circles, have had a somewhat similar effect to that which we can find in school education as resources have shifted from ministries of education to ministries of manpower. The motivations have been similar too—above all, as far as policy makers are concerned, the desire to respond to identified national needs and, as far as learners are concerned, to equip themselves with missing skills.

In such circumstances and given pressure on the institutional resources of universities and their uneven distribution, there has been an increased tendency in university institutions to become more competitive. This is in many respects a healthy response, but one which poses the long-term question, managerial but more than managerial, of the balance between competition and co-operation in higher education; competition and co-operation between universities; and competition and co-operation between universities and other institutions of higher education. Already universities are not only competing with one another or with other institutions of public higher education like polytechnics. They are facing a new kind of competition, most discussed across the Atlantic, where there has been further development in recent years which has transformed the scene—an immense increase in the volume and range of higher education provided outside educational institutions by business and by non-public organisations. The 'corporate classroom' has become a reality.

On this side of the Atlantic steps are already being taken by European multinational business to create a new institution, PACE, sharing courses already being provided in different countries in information technology and associated subjects. It is significant that much of the planning has been carried out by the Director of the European Institute of Education and Social Policy in Paris, and the experience gained is bound to have an influence on quite different fields from information technology and associated subjects. It is plain that if universities and other institutions of public higher education do not provide the kind of education which is in demand, then other agencies will attempt to do so, sometimes with larger resources at their disposal than public institutions and able in consequence to offer higher salaries and to make use of more expensive equipment. They will also have the advantage of 'newness', the kind of advantage which the new public universities of the 1960s were able to exploit. Competition will certainly be stimulated. We are familiar with its manifestations and implications within national communications systems where it is now built into the systems and where it is entering a new phase with the satellite revolution; it is less familiar within national education systems.

Historically, there was once a somewhat similar situation in relation to school education, although public education was provided to fill in gaps in the system rather than the other way round, in some countries there has been a continuing dual system, and there is new talk in Britain at least of school 'privatisation' and of the creation of new school institutions which will involve further duality. Some of the initiatives are interesting and could stimulate experiment as well as controversy if the human and financial resources on offer were adequate. Yet in the future as in the past education will demand not only long-term views but overall vision. It will be as necessary in the future as in the past to point to gaps, to compare standards, to relate limited objectives to broader objectives. For this reason the use of the word 'strategy' is as relevant in educational planning, which inevitably takes time, as it is in relation to health or to defence. Each university will have to have its strategy, but there will have to be a universities' strategy in addition: it will have to take account of pedagogy as well as of demography, of quality as well as of numbers.

The strategy would benefit from being European, and it is significant that one of the bodies most interested in the subject is the European Centre for Strategic Management of Universities with its headquarters in Brussels, which is concerned not only with university decision-making but with its social and cultural context. Other European centres, like the Institute of Work and Society in Maastricht, are also involved.

European countries with their diverse historical inheritances face common problems, although their magnitude and range vary from country to country—large-scale unemployment, related both to cyclical and structural changes; changes in the balance of work and of agriculture, industry and the service occupations; the prospect of 'leisure' for the majority on an unfamiliar and indeed, unprecedented scale; disturbed urban environment; minority pressures; ethnic misunderstanding and conflict; violence and the threat of war. Some of these problems receive more attention than others: it is interesting, for example, that there are fewer ERASMUS schemes in agriculture, at the centre of all discussions about policy in the European Community, than there are in any other subject. We have not yet adequately fitted educational policy into a social policy framework.

Meanwhile, the problems loom large and are capable of creating immediate crises. More seriously, the shapes of the twenty-first century seem less attractive to those living in the late twentieth century than the shapes of the twentieth century were for most (although not all people) living in the late nineteenth century. There was optimism that 'progress' would continue.

Now there is an undercurrent of pessimism. If there were to be an even bigger gap between the educated, who, however they are educated, are relatively secure, and the untrained, economically and socially insecure and culturally deprived, there would be far more serious problems in society than there have been before—social problems with a moral and political dimension. Their short-term implications would be disturbing, their long-term implications alarming. In place of dream there could be nightmare. Because of the social and moral dimension, any strategy of higher education will have to ensure that resources are deployed in terms of clearly defined priorities, which will take account of those who might be classified in statistical tables as 'residuals' as well as those who are talented.

It will not be enough, however, to think in terms of a strategy. Imagination will be needed as well as analysis, and effective implementation as well as shrewd forecasting. Above all, it will be necessary to communicate to large numbers of people. At present there is a communication problem in relation to higher education. Indeed, it was already there during the 1960s when in a decade of university expansion the image of universities was sometimes unappealing. It is obviously there during the 1980s when politicians sometimes seem as unsympathetic as large sections of the general public do to the mission and fate of the universities. Yet the rectification of images should no more be a simple exercise in public relations than the management of universities should simply be a simple exercise in accounting. We are dealing not only with images but with what lies behind them.

If there is misunderstanding between university vice-chancellors and their faculties on the one hand and educational policy-makers on the other, there can be no proper communication with the public. Indeed, the public will be confused, not enlightened. Equally important, there can be no effective implementation of any strategy that is devised (by either side). Those involved in higher education are in the front line, as are teachers in the school educational system. Yet while policy-makers will have to be at pains to devise 'overall' policies that will actually work, those in the front line will have to be at equal pains to prove, changing the image, that they do not constitute a vested interest resistant to all change. There will have to be considerable rethinking within the academic profession itself. There will also have to be leadership, will and drive.

It is said that in an age of advanced technology we shall need 'the wisdom of the humanities' to enhance the quality of life, and many industrialists concerned with high technology have said it. That this particular need exists is clear to any traveller through the Europe of the late-twentieth century, a Europe which makes much of its heritage. There are places on the map that need to be preserved, cultures that if they were to disappear, would leave the world deprived. Language can be an obstacle to understanding but it can also be a source of cultural strength. Music can unite where language divides. For this reason alone the European Cultural Foundation with its headquarters in Holland and generously backed by Dutch finance has a key role to play. Yet conservation is only part of the prescription that brings in the humanities. The creative imagination, which has impelled great artists—and also the greatest scientists—is characterised not so much by its wisdom—this is sometimes missing—but by its daring. In any educational strategy we are not concerned solely with limiting social risks, with meeting proven needs and with reaching agreed goals. We are mobilising the human spirit.

This is not a peroration. Indeed, perorations are out of fashion, even in *Festschrifts* presented to men of vision. It is easy to ignore profound aspects of higher education and concentrate on its instrumentalities. Yet the long history of education provides us with its own heritage of wisdom and daring. A recent conference described in the *Higher Education Newsletter* issued by the Higher Education Group of the British Higher Education Foundation was concerned with a topic entitled 'On the Maintenance of Morale in a Steady State System of Higher Education'. It is a title immediately intelligible to those concerned with academic activity. Yet it is a very limiting title. No one concerned with higher education can neglect what are called, in immediately intelligible language, 'aims and purposes', and it is in relation to 'aims and purposes' that strong voices must be heard from inside universities when educational policies are being propounded.

Europe is a continent which has mobilised the human spirit in more diverse ways than any other continent, more often, perhaps, outside universities, which were often very restricted institutions, and outside other institutions of higher education, restricted in different fashion, than inside them. What those concerned with higher education in our present phase of history can and should do is to explain why we have to concern ourselves with the past as well as with the future and why we have to cross both intellectual and geographical frontiers. As Guy Neave wrote in 1985 in the tenth anniversary issue of the *European Journal of Education*, produced by the European Institute of Education and Social Policy, the questions that 'society must ask of itself and of its higher education system' are not just 'questions of means but of ends, not of techniques but of values. They are questions that require direct dialogue between higher education and its public, not *par administration interposée*'.

JOHN MAGUIRE

3. The Case for a New Social Order*

I T is widely agreed that the Republic of Ireland is in a crisis, economically and politically. Politicians and leading opinion-makers go further, offering a diagnosis centring on the national debt, and a prescription: financial austerity 'across the board'. The diagnosis and prescription, however, flow from a world view which is seriously flawed in technical, political and moral respects; to act on it will merely intensify rather than cure the crisis. This world view is not a single, unified philosophy; there are different elements and emphases in the versions of it held by different groups. All of these groups, however, together amount to the people who have been 'in charge' in the Republic of Ireland—in so far as anyone can be 'in charge' of a modern complex society—over the last three decades. During those decades there has been much change, even some progress; but the change and the progress have not been directed by, and have poorly served, the interests of most people in the society. This is for a simple but crucial reason: the project which was launched in 1958 was one in which powerful decision-makers pursued *their* vision of what was necessary and what was possible for the society, including themselves. No effective structures existed, nor have they since emerged, for hearing the voices of 'the remainder': the voice of workers on how work should

*The author wishes to acknowledge with thanks the help and advice of many colleagues, including Garrett Barden, Dick Couto, Ciaran McCullagh, Piet Strydom, Vincent Tucker and particularly Joe Ruane.

61

be structured and organised; the voice of the poor, the low-paid, and of workers in general, on wealth and its distribution; the voice of women on male domination of society; the voice of parents, teachers and students—particularly of children—on the education system.

All of these assertions can be, and by many they will be, rejected. I believe, however, that they are increasingly well-documented, and also that they accord with the experience of large numbers of people in this society. It is only by an imaginative leap that people already in or near the centres of power can begin to see how society looks and feels to those on the receiving end. It is useless to pretend that the alternative perspective which I offer here can be 'proved' to a 'scientific' conclusion. Of course scientific argument is of the essence and I will refer to a growing body of social-scientific literature on which I rest my argument. Science, however, always operates within a deeper philosophical and ethical world view, and arguments about such world views, whilst rational in the deepest sense of the word, require a wider and more complex attention than simply 'checking out the facts'. Of course there are many 'facts', but they arise from within a given *project*, and always open the possibility of others. It is one of the secrets of social dominance that this openness should be sealed off, be hidden from the public view. The power of a socially dominant group rests not simply on controlling their subordinates' material position, but also on defining their cultural perception of the status quo and of possible alternatives to it. Politics, then, is basically about identities, and human identities are never merely given, they are always 'under construction'. I believe that the current crisis deeply challenges the definitions of identity which have been an essential ingredient of the 'modernisation project' of the last three decades in Ireland.

I am not counselling idle metaphysical speculation in the face of a very concrete crisis. I am saying that the power of leaders and opinion makers to decide who we are, where we are and where we might go from here is already shaken, and should not be restored even if it could be. Offering a statement of an alternative perspective, I do not lay claim to conclusive scientific proof, for as I have said there is not such in these affairs. I offer the perspective because first, I believe it to be true; second, I believe that it begins to articulate the situation of the 'remainders' who have been overlooked and disadvantaged by the modernisation project; third, I believe that it speaks to some of the deepest needs of groups who *do* hold sway within that project, and last, but perhaps most important of all, it offers the possibility of the democratic creation of a just, free and equal society. The alternative to this latter is, I believe, the increasingly authoritarian imposition of a set of definitions and priorities which will be asserted the more firmly and cruelly the more clearly it emerges that they are unworkable.

The Record 1958-88: Achieved Inequality

One of the major intellectual developments of the past thirty years, particularly the past decade, is the emergence of sociology as a mature discipline in its own right in Irish society. This means that it is now possible to speak with much greater confidence than hitherto of the kind of society, in all its dimensions, which we inhabit. In contributions to multi-disciplinary studies, in sociological collections and even in sociological monographs the complex picture is sketched out and coloured in. I will not attempt to summarise this impressive literature, which would very likely prove impossible. I do wish, however, to draw on it to indicate that there are very good reasons for considering an alternative perspective on the recent development of Irish society. These reasons can be briefly conveyed by taking issue with the title of one of the best known of the multi-disciplinary collections.[1]

To describe the recent past under the rubric of 'Unequal Achievement' is to suggest that overall progress has been made towards some set of communal goals but that unfortunately the achievement has not occurred equally in all social dimensions or for all social groups. In this perspective inequality is a highly worrying problem which somehow *besets* the 'achievement'; I believe rather that inequality *constitutes* the achievement. What has happened, has been the evolution of one unequal social structure into a new unequal social structure. The latter is the outcome of interaction at every stage between groups with highly unequal economic, socio-cultural and political resources. It is then not in any sense accidental that inequality has been achieved: when people act from within unequal positions and do not reflect on and correct these, what will emerge will—short of a miracle—itself be an unequal result.

My claim here is not primarily about the intentions or the goodwill of the various persons and groups involved. It is, rather, that these persons and groups have operated from material and cultural vantage-points which have become 'second nature' to their occupants, but which automatically put those with whom they interact on an inferior footing, with a consequently unequal outcome. Before indicating the structure of power through which this inequality is at once reproduced and legitimised, I wish briefly to note some of the chief aspects of the inequality itself.

It is obvious and well accepted that there has been massive change in Irish society during the economic growth of the last thirty years.

Thus, the changes in the industrial structure may be characterised as a switch from the agricultural to the industrial sector, from 'traditional' industries to more 'modern' ones, and a substantial expansion in the predominantly white collar sectors such as professional services and the public sector.[2]

While all these changes have taken place, the society has overall remained highly rigid. Rottman and O'Connell point out, it is true, that due to the decline of the agricultural sector inherited property is now a less important factor in life-chances, compared to one's ability to bargain in the labour-market. They also point out, however, that 'proprietorial' categories have *increased* as a proportion of the non-agricultural workforce. Equally the increased importance of the labour-market has not led to increased 'equality of opportunity', since access to the new positions of advantage is very largely confined to the offspring of those already occupying them. 'The result is a virtual upper middle class monopoly of the advantages that depend on education.'[3]

Peillon draws together many of the data on the distribution of economic resources. He refers to the highly unequal distribution of wealth, and to the evidence that in 1980 the top 10 per cent of income-receivers got 26.4 per cent of all income, and the top 20 per cent had 43.9 per cent, almost exactly ten times the share of the bottom 20 per cent of income-receivers who got 4.6 per cent.

> If one compares 1965-66 to 1980, it is quite clear that the poorest 50 per cent of the population disposed in 1980 of a lesser share of the national income, while the wealthier 50 per cent had improved their relative position.[4]

Rottman and O'Connell look at the impact of state transfers (i.e. taking tax and paying out benefits) on this basic structure of inequality. They conclude that 'State expenditure and taxation as experienced over the 1960s and 1970s raise questions of equity. Working-class households have increased their contribution, and proprietors and employers are taxed at a far lower rate. Middle-class employees, though paying more than the upper class, are paying less than a rigorously progressive system would require.'[5] Rottman and Hannan add the very important rider that such redistribution as does result from state policies is better understood as a transfer between families at different stages of the family life-cycle than as a transfer from richer to poorer families as such.[6]

Peillon, drawing on the work of Rottman *et al.*, gives an idea of the numerical proportions of the classes about which we are speaking. This yields a *bourgeoisie* (large proprietors including farmer-employers) of 2.2 per cent; a *petty bourgeoisie* (small proprietors and farmers) of 25.8 per cent; a *middle class* (professional intermediate and routine non-manual) of 19.2 per cent and a working class (manual and service skilled/semi-skilled/unskilled) of 43.9 per cent.[7] We can detect a definite hierarchy from the owners of large capital, through the owners of smaller property or professional skills, down to those who have only their labour power, in varying degrees of skill, to offer.

Here we encounter some crucial theoretical issues in the interpretation of the data on Irish social inequality. The first of these arises when Sammon discusses the relative fates of different groups in the three broad areas of agriculture, industry and services, stressing how certain sub-groups were marginalised during the 1960s and 1970s. He says that recent research shows that 'in the competition for adequate income positions some social classes have fared badly'.[8] This treatment implies the possibility that we could have a class system where all fared well. But classes precisely *are* unequally advantaged groups with respect to the attainment of wealth and income. Again, the emphasis on marginalisation might imply that, apart from these victims, things are all right. But 'marginal' groups stand to the other members of their class as do the casualties to the survivors in an army—they just happen to be the ones who were hit!

The second major theoretical issue concerns how we conceive of the top, rather than the bottom, of the class hierachy. I raise this issue with humility, as a social theorist increasingly aware of the debt he owes to the research which has uncovered so much about inequality in this society in recent decades. It is offered in the hope of promoting a further creative interaction between basic theory and factual inquiry. To read many social scientists, one would think that we were back in late feudal/early capitalist society, with the bourgeoisie as a 'middle class' between the lower orders on the one hand and the landed aristocracy on the other. Thus Rottman and O'Connell, as we have seen, suggest lumping employers in with the major professions and managers to constitute 'the upper middle class'.[9] Peillon similarly tells us that: 'there are three major socially differentiated groupings in the Republic of Ireland: the farmers, the working class and the broadly defined urbanised middle class.'[10] He then proceeds to *divide* the 'middle class' into bourgeoisie, petty bourgeois, professionals and office workers. At least, on this conception, the bourgeoisie get to be 'top of the middle class'.

Whelan and Whelan are more direct, and I would suggest more correct when they speak of an upper class *tout court*.[11] One interesting recent development is the study of the 1987 general election, in which three political scientists found that:

> First, the class basis of Irish politics is more evident now than at any time in the previous twenty years. Second, when we refine our conception of class, the class basis of politics comes into even sharper focus.'[12]

The more refined class picture which they employ, and which they find to be more effective, distinguishes bourgeoisie, petty bourgeoisie, middle class and working class, and then farmers (large and small). They seem, along with Whelan and Whelan, to accept the basic truth that you can have a 'middle' only where there is a top!

There is more than definitional purism at stake here. Very

many studies on Irish society over the past few decades have employed categories drawn broadly from the Marxist and Weberian traditions, as developed for example by Anthony Giddens.[13] Yet many of the social scientists employing these categories seem extraordinarily coy about accepting the reality of capitalist domination, *which is as much part of Weber's notion of modern industrial society as it is of Marx's*. This is not to say that the two conceptions are identical, for Weber introduces major refinements as regards types of property and of marketable skill; but these are differences *within* a shared acceptance of first, the centrality of class to modern social inequality and second, the centrality of capitalist property in the modern class system. Even for reasons of intellectual consistency, we need to follow out the logic of the schemes we employ or devise new categories—Ilium may have had its 'topless towers', but modern Irish society is not so endowed.

To say this is not to suggest that the incumbents of the dominant socio-economic positions in Irish society would necessarily qualify for a 'Guaranteed Irish' label. It is becoming increasingly clear that the process of Irish capitalist development is articulated with the development of the world capitalist system. Therefore one cannot give an account of the structure of Irish society, in class or any other terms, without major reference to its increasingly explicit involvement with the capitalist international economic order. An awareness both of capitalist domination and of its increasingly international character, would lead us to greet with some caution the observation of Rottman and O'Connell that:

> The determination of life-chances has over the past twenty-five years become for the most part self contained within Ireland: The workforce no longer spans the Irish Sea, emigration has virtually ceased, and demography has been shaped by natural increase and immigration.[14]

Quite clearly Rottman and O'Connell would recast this judgment now, in the light of the return of emigration in the five years since they wrote. But my basic quarrel with their assessment could have been made in 1982, without any reference to emigration whatsoever. This is, that the process which they are describing was underpinned by a new *openness* of the Irish economy to international investment, so that in a sense Ireland was becoming, not more 'self-contained' as such, but a somewhat more 'dynamic' and 'self-contained' local branch of global capitalism. In the five years since Rottman and O'Connell wrote, emigration has re-emerged as central to Irish social experience, along with an increase in unemployment from 150,000 in 1982 to 240,982 in December 1987.[15] These I would argue are both symptoms of the fragility of the underlying industrialisation strategy of recent decades. This brings us to the question of the nature of the process of social change since independence, and particularly since 1958.

The Bourgeois Modernisation Project and Irish Development

Peillon tells us that:

> In any event to catalogue social changes in Ireland under the single label of *modernisation* does not get us very far. The real question does not concern the transition from the traditional to the modern but rather the model of modernity itself which Ireland assumes, and, more concretely, the identification of the forces and struggles through which each strives to direct and control the process of modernisation.[16]

Peillon is here presenting 'modernisation' as a general abstract category which is then concretely specified by social forces. There is however another perspective, which sees modernisation as precisely the process of incorporation of a

69

not-yet-industrialised society, region or group into the capitalist world system. This process is overseen, in so far as conscious effective direction is concerned, by a dominant coalition of social forces united by their orientation to the requirements of capital in an international context. Given this, I have no quarrel with Peillon's account of the actual 'ingredients' of the project which has taken place in Ireland:

> The State project is richer and more complex than that of the bourgeoisie, which it embraces as its central element without being smothered by it.[17]

Peillon himself makes it very clear that many details have to be added to the broad picture of social and political power which he has provided. We can however say with confidence that there is a separate stratum where key policies have been developed, and key decisions taken, in Irish society. We may also say with confidence that workers (including the unemployed), small farmers, most women, children and the various categories of 'the poor' are excluded from it. Equally, owners of businesses and of large farms, senior managers (of private business in all sectors, and of public enterprise) and senior civil servants and politicians are in it. This stratum is quite close to Tovey's depiction of 'a corporate élite extending into agri-business, industrial, commercial and political circles'.[18] The precise configuration and limits of the stratum may alter, and equally it may need to be differently construed on specific issues; the Catholic Church and the senior professions may have their ambiguous liaisons with it, and the leadership of the labour movement may have become more or less incorporated with it as (very subsidiary) 'social partners'. All of these questions need further treatment, and great progress has been made in treating some of them already. What I am concerned to do here is, centrally, to contribute to a wider discussion by isolating and critiquing some key aspects of the world view, and the managerial culture, of this stratum.

70

It is true, of course, that Ireland has never seen a united, self-confident and cohesive national bourgeoisie; this is as true for the whole island, before and after partition, as it is for the southern Irish bourgeoisie. Yet the 'peculiarities' of Irish development have enhanced, at least as much as they have diminished, the viability of bourgeois-nationalist rhetoric and ideology. For example, there is the powerful cultural frame set by a nationalist struggle in the late nineteenth and early twentieth centuries, in which a highly authoritarian Catholic Church, commanding allegiance from almost all social levels and classes, came to prominence. There also emerged a socially powerful state bureaucracy, inheriting both structure and styles of authoritarianism from the British colonial system. These and other factors combined to lend a centrality and ideological weight to the requirements of capitalist industry, far beyond the capacity of the bourgeoisie itself to promote growth and provide employment. It was an explicable, but not an inevitable development.

There could have emerged, for example, a fascist-corporate state founded in a reactionary interpretation of Catholic social teaching, or even—less probably—a populist state capitalism directed by a coalition between the more radical elements of the revolutionary nationalist movement and a more 'socially-oriented' central bureaucracy. I mention these alternative scenarios simply to dispel the impression of inevitability which always wafts around what actually happened. Given, though, that it did emerge as the centre-piece of Irish economic and social developments since partition, it is not surprising that the bourgeoisie found in both Church and State such authoritative champions of its basic assumptions. It is those assumptions which are called in question by the current crisis, which can best be described as a crisis of the bourgeois modernisation project of the last thirty years.

Modernisation is an enormously complex concept, which becomes more complex the more closely one looks at it. Indeed there may be a basis for calling it an 'essentially contested concept', which has very little 'neutral' meaning, apart from the conflicting theories applied to it.[19] It is also too often forgotten that modernisation theory has its roots in, and stands or falls with, a particular account of how capitalism *came to be* in the already-developed heartland. This is the theory of 'Industrial Society', which emphasises the enlightened, scientific, consensual and functional aspects of industrial development, playing down the elements of ideology, domination, conflict and exploitation emphasised by theories of 'Capitalist Society'.[20] If 'modernisation' is false as both a description of and a prescription for less developed countries, this is in large part because it is false as a description of how developed countries got to where they are, and of their present structure and process.

In this context, Commins gives a very useful account of how two alternative theories, 'modernisation' and 'structural' theory, would apply to recent Irish rural development. Without taking a simple-minded view that one perspective can be simply proved 'true' while the other is demonstrably 'false', Commins indicates very powerfully those features of Irish rural development which would call for a 'structural' rather than a 'modernisation' explanation.

> Rural or regional poverty, therefore, is not an anachronism in the modern world but is in fact created—however unintentionally—by policies of modern economic development. Thus, the basic causes of underdevelopment are not the cultural characteristics of people but the character of the main structures and institutions—the economy, government, the law, etc. These institutions are seen to be maintained because they serve the ideologies and class interests of those who control power and economic resources.[21]

Wickham is even more forthright in rejecting the notion that what has taken place in the Republic of Ireland over the last few decades can be described neutrally as 'industrialisation'. He turns to the theory of dependency as an alternative to modernisation theory pointing out that dependency theory can make good sense of the two main phases of Irish industrial experience since independence. The first phase up to 1958 provides 'an almost classical example of a dependent society in the sense outlined by Frank'. On the other hand, the growth which has taken place since 1958, he tells us, 'seems in turn to be a clear example of dependent industrialisation'.[22] Of course, there are some alternatives to modernisation theory; along with dependency theory in its various guises, we have mode of production theory and radical political economy to name but two; equally, the work of applying such alternatives to the characterisation of recent Irish development is still incomplete. For the purposes of this present discussion, however, it is sufficient to note that the 'modernisation' account of recent decades is highly questionable, and that there is a good basis for working out an alternative around central notions of power, exploitation and ideology. One important contribution is that of Holland, who locates the development of Irish society in the overall context of the successive phases of world capitalism. I see much truth in his overall judgment that:

> Ireland may now be engaging with modernisation in the world economy, precisely at the point when modernisation itself is coming into profound crisis.[23]

Holland builds his analysis around the distinction between three successive phases of world capitalist development: the nineteenth-century era of laisser-faire, the development of the welfare state, at least in the capitalist heartlands, from the 1930s to the 1970s, and the present phase which he describes as that of 'the National Security State'. This latter evolves through pressures from international capital within the state in question, for (1) cheap wages, (2) low taxes/subsidies to encourage investment, (3) increased state military capacity and (4) internal political stability. Although I will not expand on it here, I believe that the concept of the national security state is a very useful framework in which to make sense of many recent Irish developments, not only those in and relating to the North of Ireland but equally those involved in the recent referendum on the 'security' implications of Title III of the Single European Act.[24]

I will conclude this section by proposing that the process in which the Republic of Ireland has been involved over the past three decades has been one of an increasingly open involvement with, and response to, the requirements of international investment capital. It has been a 'modernisation project' in two senses: first, that it has brought about new structures, and to an extent new attitudes, in the place of traditional ones, and second, in the sense that, for a complex of reasons, both state and bourgeoisie have presented and justified it under the technical, consensual rubric of 'industrial society' and played down its political, conflictual features. In the remainder of this essay I wish to point to fundamental defects in the value system and managerial culture which go along with this project, and to argue that we can and must begin to articulate a new set of values and an alternative project. Central to all of this discussion will be the problem of the operation of power in capitalist society.

Capitalism and Power: An Underview

It is as true in political and social life as it is in scientific methodology that all theories are underdetermined by data. What this means is that there is nothing in life, including science itself, which can be exhaustively validated on 'pure scientific' grounds, at least in the usual empirical/experimental understanding of scientific procedure. This is part of the complex meaning of Marx's statement that:

> The ideas of the ruling class are in every epoch the ruling ideas: i.e. the class which is the ruling *material* force of society, is at the same time its ruling *intellectual* force. The individuals composing the ruling class possess among other things consciousness and therefore think. Insofar, therefore, as they rule as a class and determine the extent and compass of an epoch, it is self-evident that they do this in its whole range, hence among other things rule also as thinkers, as producers of ideas, and regulate the production and distribution of the ideas of their age: Thus their ideas are the ruling ideas of the epoch.[25]

Marx here is clearly providing not just some brute 'correlation' between material and cultural dominance: he is giving us a theoretical account of how the former both requires and makes possible the latter. It is essential for a dominant class to be able to articulate, from within its own ideological perspective, an 'acceptable version' of the needs and interests of other classes within society.[26] The life-process of Irish society has been articulated in this manner within a broadly bourgeois ideology or world view; it is this world view which the current crisis most centrally calls in question.

One cannot transform—even *re*form—a social order by mere social fantasising; it is essential to have a coherent alternative account of the present condition and possible future development of the society. Equally, however, it is extremely salutary to realise that the bourgeois world view is, ultimately, just one account of society, personality and history. It is of such great importance in world history, of course, because the bourgeoisie have been able to 'mobilise' human and natural resources on such an unprecedented scale over the last few centuries. But if this is true, it follows that the secret of the success of bourgeois ideas is, *not* their inherent 'rightness' by some supra-historical criterion, but precisely their hold on the crucial economic, political and cultural resources of society. The success of bourgeois ideology arises from and vitally reinforces the bourgeois mobilisation of society; as the mobilisation becomes evidently more problematic, it behoves us to criticise the ideology.

Whilst we need to retain a healthy scepticism about the ability of 'ideology-critique' to transform social orders on its own, we need also to realise both its crucial importance and its enormous difficulty. If the perspective from which this essay is written is valid, then we need deeply to examine the 'normality' which we have come to take for granted, and within which all our endeavours, social-scientific and other, have been conducted. This requires an alternative account of the history of the last few centuries, in terms not of 'modernisation' and 'industrialism', but of 'conflict' and 'capitalism'. I shall not attempt to provide such an account here, but I do want to focus on one particular aspect, namely that of power.

A brief discussion of the different faces of power, as they are depicted in the notorious 'Community Power Debate', is a useful way of pursuing our critical reflections. In response to the 'élite' theories of C. Wright Mills and Floyd Hunter, the pluralists, led by Robert Dahl, put forward a behavioural, 'scientific' approach. This focused on the actual *issues* discussed within a given political system, and concluded that these were handled by a 'plurality' of leaderships rather than a single, coherent élite. But Bachrach and Baratz were quick to point out that, as well as the power which decides on issues, there is a 'second face of power' which decides what will be the issues, and what will remain mere *'grievances'* outside the political arena. Stephen Lukes was equally quick to do to Bachrach and Baratz what they did to Dahl—he pointed out a 'third face of power'. The effect of this third face of power is that only certain items even become grievances, while some remain mere '*problems*' of which many of their victims are as such unaware.[27]

These notions of power can be applied, for example, to the discussion of social and economic policy in contemporary Ireland. The national debt is quite clearly an issue—it is the focal point of explicit, public political discussion, and positions are taken on precisely how to deal with it. But there is apparently only one basic approach to be taken to this issue, namely financial cutbacks, because we are told that 'increased taxation is simply not an option'. The discussion of the taxation system classically illustrates how:

> demands for change in the existing allocation of benefits and privileges in the community can be suffocated before they are even voiced; or kept covert; or killed before they gain access to the relevant decision-making arena; or, failing all these things, maimed or destroyed in the decision-implementing stage of the policy process.[28]

In so far as taxation does surface as an issue at all, it does so within very definite limits. First of all there is the oft repeated assertion that 'we' in general are paying too much tax. Then, and only then, is the excessive share of actual taxation borne by the PAYE sector adverted to. In this way, the general resentment that anyone feels at having to pay something rather than nothing is translated into a cross-class alliance against 'excessive taxation'. This, in a situation where taxes on wealth or capital are described by one authority as having 'drifted towards the inconsequential',[29] and by another as 'virtually non-existent'.[30] The net result is that those who should be paying no tax at all, or much less than they do pay, are co-opted into a 'general anti-tax alliance' by those on high salaries and/or with large holdings of wealth, who should be paying far more towards a more progressive system, in every sense of the word.

If PAYE taxation hovers uneasily on the threshold between mere grievances and public issues, the distribution of income and wealth is barely perceived *even* as a grievance: it is treated to the third face of power and for the most part remains merely a 'problem' of which most people most of the time are unaware. It would be ridiculous to pretend that top salary-earners and property-owners wake up every morning saying 'What will we do to deceive them today?' But it would be even more ridiculous to overlook the huge wall of secrecy which exists around the distribution of our basic resources. A large part of the energies of our banking, legal and accounting professions goes to ensure precisely that *no one* will know who owns what. There has been a Commission on Taxation, but none on the distribution of income and wealth; unofficial studies exist on income-distribution, but virtually nothing on the distribution of wealth. Academic social science has been just as much a 'victim' of this manipulation as has been our political process. Thus there now exist few, if any, of the data from which one could propose a redistributive alternative to the current financial cut-backs. But this works both ways: if there *is* a 'consensus' at present on taxation and distribution in Irish society, it is one which has been grotesquely manipulated by the well-off and the highly-paid. It provides neither a technical nor a moral foundation for conclusions such as T.K. Whitaker's that 'it must be accepted that the scope for re-distribution is limited'.[31]

Power and Identity: from Leprechauns to We-Folk

In the context of notions of power and agenda-control, it is not surprising that the rhetoric of Irish modernisation has been shot through with references to the betterment of 'our' situation and with prescriptions as to what 'we' should do to achieve this. Modern capitalist society differs from traditional, feudal society precisely in its need to articulate itself through 'universal' values. The enlightenment project, which was such a powerful bourgeois weapon against medievalism, both required and expressed an explicit dependence of the bourgeoisie on lower social classes in their rise to dominance. The bourgeoisie were in every way obliged to call on the masses to defeat the ecclesiastical, monarchical and aristocratic powers of late feudal society. In terms of both its culture and its economic structure, bourgeois society required the active involvement of the lower orders, and it had to proclaim universal, egalitarian values to achieve this.

One of the most powerful illusions of the bourgeoisie is that their project is uniquely and conclusively 'scientific'. Once the 'age of industry' was properly launched, then all discord could be regarded as 'teething problems', or 'growing pains' on the road to social 'maturity'. The flavour of such breezy technicism, Irish style, is forever captured for me by one of the covers of *Time* magazine. In the week of John F. Kennedy's visit here in June of 1963, it showed (as I recall) a lace curtain with shamrock motif being drawn back by a leprechaun. The scene revealed was the new and shining Ireland of brightly burnished high-technology factories: the metal fist in the shamrock glove. By implication, the leprechaun was performing his last official function, passing the torch, in Kennedy's words, to a new generation. This new generation would apply the truths of science, not the myths of tradition, to building a new world of peace, progress and prosperity.

The practical reality of the last twenty-five to thirty years has sadly belied this bright promise. This is so not only in terms of concrete social experience, but also in terms of the rhetorical style of leaders and opinion makers. For the new Ireland of the bourgeois modernisation project has proved to have its own contemporary myths, as the leprechauns mutated into their bourgeois variant, the 'We-Folk'. The strength of this myth may be indicated by attempting to write even a simple page about the current crisis of Irish society without using 'we', 'us' or 'our'. I have done it at the start of this article and it proved extremely and instructively difficult. I am not cynically rejecting the notion of political and social community—rather am I emphasising that such a community is a rare and precious achievement, the result of a process of the creation of political and social identity. To say that this process has not been undertaken in Irish society is a gross understatement—it has been, and is, systematically avoided by those very leaders and opinion-makers who speak to 'us' of 'our' society and crisis. 'We' have not been anywhere or done anything, nor are 'we' going anywhere, because 'we' quite simply do not exist. With the deepest cynicism, the language of community has been used to prevent the reality of community: if 'we' once took ourselves seriously, 'we' would start to ask: 'What and where are our resources? What are our shared possibilities? What is the significance of different social roles and positions in relation to our overall welfare?' These are all questions which the decision-making stratum quite simply cannot face, and cannot allow to become real for their subordinates. They cannot do so, because their position of economic, social and political dominance would immediately be threatened.

One of our most enthusiastic modernisers has told us:

> The maturity of a culture, no less than of an individual, is reflected in the urge to search for, and the capacity to confront the truth about itself. Behind its sober prose, *Economic Development* extended an invitation to Irish society to embark on a search for self-knowledge, and not to flinch from the findings.[32]

This is the best description I know, *per contra*, of what *did not* happen in Irish society in 1958, and has certainly not happened since. It strains credulity, to say the least, when we are told that a government publication could be regarded as an 'invitation' to a 'society' to embark on anything. I have no objection to people's holding strong views on alternative policies within the top decision-making stratum, but I object strongly to anyone's confusing the conduct of such debates with democracy. If, as is reasonable, we single out *Economic Development* as the symbol of a new outlook, then that outlook merely gave to the various élites something new to say to their subordinates. It was an exercise in 'top-down planning' on the grand scale. If 'self-knowledge' had been acquired by 'Irish society', it would have involved precisely a critique *not* of the beliefs of our decision-making élites, but of the very notion that 'our' affairs should be decided by an élite in the first place. So much for 'cultural maturity'—the *really* 'distasteful challenge' is that of breaking down the self-justifying ideological defences of bourgeois bureaucracy, of confronting the contempt for ordinary people which is so deep-rooted in modern managerial culture. That challenge, which questions the very culture of domination itself, was never confronted, and now stares 'us' in the face.

I am aware that this viewpoint will be greeted with incredulity by some, and with impatience by others; such naïve abstractions, I will be told, are out of place when there is serious and urgent work to be done. But all work requires definitions of just what the task is, of who should carry it out, how and why. Such definitions have almost never been considered in Irish society; instead, recourse is had to the contemporary myth of the 'We Folk'. The decision-making stratum are faced with mobilising large numbers of people in pursuit of objectives which have never been scrutinised in anything like a real democratic political forum. They also face the problem of *demobilising* increasing thousands of those same people now that 'economic reality' denies them a role and a livelihood. It is salutary to consider the enormous contribution made to this tight-rope act by that innocent entity, the first person plural. When financial austerity is to be the order of the day, 'we' have spent 'ourselves' into a crisis. When profits are under threat, 'we' are in danger of pricing 'ourselves' out of the market. When social welfare services are cut back, 'we' have to tighten 'our' belts. This repressive mythology has a particular hold in a society, like Ireland, where there is a strongly authoritarian religious and political culture, with little established tradition of public dissent. It can be articulated negatively as well as positively: those who today are part of 'us' will tomorrow be outcasts, condemned for 'holding society to ransom'.

In this context it is not surprising that a number of writers have recently commented on the prevalence of *silence* in Irish society. Senator Brendan Ryan has criticised the response of our social welfare system to the current crisis of unemployment. Indeed, his analysis could be seen as yet another classic illustration of agenda-control *á la* Bachrach and Baratz:

> So you have the 'lazy unemployed' myth, the well fostered view that most people could get a job if they really wanted … With public sympathy deluded it is easy to keep the unemployed quiet… The system has thus forced unemployed people into a role which demands idleness, silence and passivity.'[33]

The close links between power and silence are also indicated by Sammon:

> It could be said that over the past two decades a key question has been silently resolved without ever having been publicly debated, *viz.* 'whose participation can we do without?'[34]

O'Carroll, analysing the role of 'community' in Irish political culture, suggests that the style of political discourse leaves 'little room for the mundane in public discourse. As a result there are large areas of silence in public life.'[35]

Perhaps most significantly of all, Curtin and Varley, having surveyed the literature on childhood in Ireland, from the 1930s to the 1970s, note:

> One continuity . . . is the finding that silence and passivity continue to be the most desired qualities in young farm children.[36]

It is in childhood that the message of fear or of openness, of possibility or of resignation, is crucially imprinted in our minds. Here again the Irish experience is but a particular version of a repressiveness that lies deep within contemporary culture. There may be no audible difference between the silence of need fulfilled and that of need suppressed; between the two, however, lies a world of possibility denied.[37]

Conclusion: Towards a New Project

There is an urgent need for a new project for Irish society. It will emerge only if it answers to perceived needs and possibilities. Equally however it will require a conscious political choice and action on the part of many persons and groups, particularly those at present most removed from the centres of power. Some elements for an alternative are to hand, in the various critiques of current policies and of their assumptions.[38] There are also indications that the political hold of the established conservative parties is less secure than their present Dáil representation might suggest. Through all the complexities of the campaign—economic versus foreign policy, positive choice versus protest vote, and so on—the referendum on the Single European Act in 1987 showed that 30 per cent of voters were prepared to reject the establishment line, despite a barrage of economic threats and blandishments.

A vital ingredient in elaborating an alternative to the current conventional wisdom is the posing of radically new questions. The severe disequilibrium of current policies, their massive failure to provide and to convince, is camouflaged by a deeper perception of their inevitability: bad and all as they are, they are based on 'the facts'. The dismissal of dissident voices as 'irresponsible' and 'dangerous' wears ever more thin in the face of the dangerous irresponsibility (in every sense) of current orthodoxy. Yet that orthodoxy will always win by default so long as it is conceded that it represents 'reality', however painful. An essential step towards dislodging it is to point out, as Senator Brendan Ryan has so well put it, that 'the so-called objectivity is the self-righteousness of an establishment determined to preserve privilege.'[39]

This critique must begin where radical bourgeois critique tails off into silence. In his assessment of society and culture from the '50s to the '80s, Lee observes that 'research might appear to be urgently required into those alien beings, "people".' He goes on to suggest that *values* will be a crucial area of study, pointing out that the OECD sees the study of values as 'a rewarding investment, even by the most mercenary criteria'. Within less than a page, he is bewailing the 'extraordinarily uneven range of ability' within Irish decision-making élites.

> This increases the urgency of making the most effective use of scarce talent and of removing obstructionists.[40]

Max Weber could hardly have hoped for a better illustration of bourgeois rationality's inability to confront questions of value *as such*. No sooner has Lee opined that values—i.e., what we do and why we do it—are important, than he hurries on to the question of how we do things. In Weber's terms, Lee broaches the question of *substantive* rationality but, finding this intractable, retreats to questions of *technical* or *formal* rationality.[41]

84

All this is far from accidental. The bourgeois project, whilst proclaiming universal values, rests ultimately in material class domination. Its invocation of values serves far less to orient society towards the fulfilment of these values than to distract from their systematic non-fulfilment. The ritual invocation of 'values' as a prelude to the call for greater 'efficiency' is thus the outer limit, the 'edge of the envelope' of the bourgeois intellectual trajectory; beyond that limit the oxygen of bourgeois certitude becomes too thin; and life as 'we' know it can no longer be sustained.

But value-questions are neither the mere abstractions, nor the lurking menaces, which they represent to the bourgeois mind. They raise the suppressed realities and possibilities of the status quo. The present set of policies, and the institutions from which they emerge, are not our only possibilities, and it is very hard to believe that they are the best. They need to be calmly, consistently and clearly challenged, in the name of an emerging way of life which can be truly available to all, rather than the preserve of a dominant élite.

Of course the need for, and attractions of, such a project will be far from obvious to most of the bourgeoisie and to many of those who currently administer society. But that is not a predetermined inevitability. Although they cannot be elaborated here, there are good grounds for arguing that the bourgeois project itself fundamentally damages the 'haves' as well as the 'have-nots'. Writers like Klaus Theweleit have cast light on the profound *fear* which has lain at the heart of that project since its emergence in the late medieval era.

Like every dominant force that wishes to remain dominant, feudal capitalism (followed by bourgeois capitalism and the bourgeois state) took up the task of blocking new possibilities, obscuring their existence, chaining them up, redirecting streams for their own benefit, 'codifying' them in a way that served dominant

85

interests, yet allowed subject peoples to retain the illusion of newfound freedom.[42]

Behind the direct, obvious repression and exclusion of subordinates 'because there isn't enough to go round' lies an even deeper and more powerful urge: the fear of losing an identity defined in terms of possessive dominance. Thus the material social contradictions of capitalism are parallelled by an equally significant cultural tension, between those 'of' society and those merely 'in' it.[43] Hegel was one of the first to show, with his Master and Slave dialetic, the inherent self-defeating insecurity of such a stance. His theme is taken up in Marx's assertion that:

> The propertied class and the class of the proletariat present the same human self-alienation. But the former class finds in this self-alienation its confirmation and its good, its own power: it has in it a semblance of human existence.[44]

There is emerging an ever more urgent choice between, on the one hand, an increasingly narrow and exclusive assertion of the bourgeois way of life for those who can 'make it', leaving the remainder to the dole-queue, the prison and the psychotropic drugs and, on the other hand, a creative recasting of our already abundant resources into a new pattern. It is quite simply the case that modern industrial civilisation has the resources to feed, clothe and shelter not only the population of Ireland but indeed that of the whole world. Every year 'we' spend roughly as much on armaments as the entire debt burden of Third World countries. The major obstacle to the creation of a humane world is certainly not some inherent technical difficulty, but the power of those 'irresponsible minorities' that have been so eloquently castigated by ex-President Luis Echeverria of Mexico.[45]

Whilst it would be absurd to expect mass conversion of

the bourgeoisie, or of their managerial and intellectual cohorts, it is salutary to reflect on the flight from human reality that lies at the very heart of their project. This may not move them to embrace new possibilities, but it helps to loosen the mesmeric power of their world-view on others. That is an important step to the emergence of a new project. Intellectuals in particular may hope to play a role in this process, even if it is chiefly the negative contribution of con-testing, of silencing, the current orthodoxy. It would be at best ridiculous, at worst extremely damaging, to try to 'speak for the oppressed'. We can simply create a forum where those who have spoken only in private bitterness, or not at all, may speak in public debate.

If ordinary people, those at present excluded from power, find their voice, then the questions which bedevil the radical intellectual—such as 'reform' versus 'revolution', or 'values' versus 'efficiency'—will be resolved as practical, political issues. If not, then all will remain, in Marx's chilling phrase, matters for purely scholastic dispute.[46] The reclaiming of discourse will involve something far more, and quite other, than merely the negation of bourgeois cer-titudes. As there is an asymmetry between life viewed from the top down and from the bottom upwards, so the voices of 'the remainder' will speak of things undreamt-of—or *only* dreamt-of—in bourgeois culture:

Here, the dams break. Curiosity swims upstream and turns around, surprising itself. Desire streams forth through the channels of imagination. Barriers—between women and men, the 'high' and the 'low'—crumble in the face of this new energy. This is what the fascist held himself in horror of, and what he saw in communism, in female sexuality—a joyous commingling, as disorderly as life. In this fantasy, the body expands, in its senses, its imaginative reach—to fill the earth. And we are at last able to rejoice in the softness and the permeability of the

87

world around us, rather than holding ourselves back in lonely dread. This is the fantasy that makes us, both men and women, human—and makes us, sometimes, revolutionaries in the cause of life.[47]

PETER FROGGATT

4. Business and Academia–
the Fruitful Interaction of
Town and Gown

INTRODUCTION

IT is a commonplace that 'enterprise'* in business, especially in large corporations, is not generated exclusively
by the career-orientated professional but draws on the
experience, knowledge, perceptions and perspectives of a
wide spectrum of expertise and, hopefully, wisdom. The
more complex and diversified the enterprise, the more is this
true. These wider views are not expressed in the boardroom
through the impersonality of the written word, the
uninvolved pedagogy of the infrequent instructional
seminar, or the anarchic framework of the 'participatory
brain-storming' session, but in a more regular way through
discussion and debate which, to be effective, demands above
all committed and regular involvement from all members of
the board. Such joint participation in policy-making of prac-
titioners in a wide range of disciplines and interests adds
immediacy, direction and relevance to their various and
often disparate viewpoints which enables fruitful debate
and, as theory and often practice bear out, a more reasoned

*I use 'enterprise' here in its dictionary meaning of a readiness to engage in an
undertaking, especially a bold or difficult one, rather than the narrower meaning
found, for example, in the pioneer work by Thorstein Veblen, The Theory of
Business Enterprise, New York: Scribner's, 1912.

89

and often more effective final policy. This *rationale* is not confined to commerce: thus, as well as in the boardrooms of public and often larger private companies, disparate walks of life are represented on the governing bodies of many chartered institutions—such as universities, on statutory bodies—such as health boards, or legislative assemblies—such as wholly or partly nominated upper houses in bicameral constitutions (in lower houses also but through self-selection and the whim of the electorate), and on central and regional advisory and deliberative bodies. The objectives of the enterprises and the mechanisms of board appointments may be dissimilar but the reasons for such heterogenity of interest are not. Only the naïve or innocent, however, would suppose that this broad church is unconnected with self-interest or the public's appetite for 'representation' and the exercise of executive power—for example, the non-elective seats in Seanad Eireann (or the non-hereditary ones in the House of Lords) and the nominees on public bodies can scarcely be typified by the average man in the street, while non-executive directors on boards of companies are chosen for what they can contribute, not for whom or what they may be seen to represent. In short, the enshrining of these practices in the constitution, law, code, or articles of association of an enterprise represents a compromise between what the executive may want and what the regulatory or sovereign authority, and ultimately the public, may require or at least be prepared to accept.

The niceties of all this are for the corporate lawyer and not for the management *dilettante* authoring this essay. Instead, I wish to examine: *first*, the contribution that an academic can make to the corporate business sector and its enterprise, particularly in large public companies, and the contribution a businessman can make to a tertiary level educational body and *its* enterprise; *second*, the practical and conceptual problems which each faces in the other's corporate environment; and *third*, the problems of a non-executive director of whatever background in generating enterprise in his company. What follows has no pretence at scholarly treatment. I have hardly left even my footprint on the mountain of germane material. It is, however, based on experience in both camps, straddling the period when university structures were lauded as the guardian of liberal values, and the university ethos as their epitome, and that of the present-day when university and business sectors are alike criticised as unenterprising and inadequate, even obstructive, to the social, economic, educational, political and, for all I know, also the spiritual, well-being of British and Irish society.

THE WORLD OF THE ACADEMIC

When an academic enters the world of business he enters an alien culture; those from universities, the dominant and most influential though not the largest constituent of the sector, probably experiencing the culture shock most acutely. To an extent greater than polytechnics (or National Institutes of Higher Education), technical colleges (or Regional Technical Colleges and others), or other tertiary colleges, all of which combine degree and non-degree courses or offer the latter alone, and are in the main 'vocationally' orientated, universities exist to advance and impart knowledge. They are also authorised to award their own degrees. They therefore have a clear 'mission', defined 'objectives', and a unique authority, properties easily translatable into commercial 'enterprise' terms. They are not, be it noted, designed specifically for anything else; certainly not to accommodate the demands of commerce, still less to be the engines of national regeneration. To *advance* knowledge does not require corporate trappings, on-line management, centralised authority, or a strategic plan: indeed to adopt

91

these implies selecting priorities, focusing on corporate objectives and marshalling resources towards their achievement, as well as demanding company discipline, all of which have been historically considered unnecessary and are anathema to the individual careers and objectives of university staff since few know at outset which of their research activities will be successful or important, still less memorable and durable, and in any event staff loyalty is to subject and scholarship, not to any corporate body. The idea of 'classified information' or 'commercial — in confidence' is alien to university and academic alike: 'reserved areas' in university business are almost exclusively to do with staff preserves against student encroachment, and internal personnel matters. To *impart* knowledge *does* require some unit and corporate management, and this admittedly is often lacking. Learning can be an end in itself but is now usually geared to the award of a degree or diploma which allows the graduate or diplomate to enter some socially useful and remunerated profession much to society's advantage—and of course his own. This so-called 'service station' role is often seen as a modern function. This is not so; it is as old as universities themselves, as witness their role in training the medieval intellectual élite—clerics, lawyers, doctors, and the secular administrative class, at times generously leavened with the froth of the more hedonistic sons of courtiers and territorial grandees. It is neither accident nor merely a convenient categorisation of the corpus of existing knowledge that the medieval faculties were Theology, Law, Medicine and Arts.

A university must be organised to discharge these functions, with the 'advancement of knowledge' paramount. This is best arranged by diffusing, not concentrating authority, the antithesis of the commercial enterprise, though this is not always good practice for the 'imparting knowledge' part of a university's activities. Its governing body is large, unwieldy, unpaid and uninvolved; not unjustly seen as a rubber stamp. Its members are either elected representatives (not necessarily the most able available) of the graduate body and of the staff, mainly academic but increasingly also of the well-unionised non-academic staff, or they are nominees of society's power blocs and the state. Occasionally there are one or two student members: in Queen's University, Belfast, for example, there has been a student member (if a graduate: 'in attendance' if an undergraduate) since 1908; two members, graduate or otherwise, since 1982. This is hardly the stuff of boards of directors, closer indeed to Gilbert and Sullivan's House of Peers (in *Iolanthe*) who 'throughout the years, did nothing in particular but did it very well'. (Harsher critics would add the next stanza where 'they showed no pretence at intellectual eminence, nor scholarship sublime'). University government bodies have one transcendent requirement—a lay (non-staff) majority: trumpeted as the conduit of wide sectoral advice it exists in fact to ensure the ultimate check on the staff's well-known exuberant propensity to spend! In no way does the governing body see itself as exercising corporate power or fostering 'enterprise'. Its chairman is a figurehead *de facto*; of the decision implementors and heads of divisions, only the vice-chancellor ('chief academic and administrative officer'; 'executive' and 'manager' are not known to most universities' statutes) is *ex officio* a member. The policy-making and management-assessment impotence of the governing body is compounded by the fact that purely academic matters (such as curricula, examinations, student admissions and discipline, appointing examiners, i.e. the main means of discharging the university's *raison d'étre*) are controlled by another body—the medieval *Senatus Academicus* consisting exclusively of academic staff with a minority of students—on the ground that the laity on the governing body must be kept at arms' length from making

93

decisions on academic matters, else they will introduce the worst of their tainted worlds into the purities of scholarly rectitude, a view amply supported by events both past and present, here and abroad. This division of responsibility ensures a substantial autonomy for academic staff, often indeed for individuals or small groups given the nature of academic work, dichotomises the institution's command structure, disperses decision-taking and strategic planning, and makes financial control difficult. Members of governing bodies sometimes react against such a supine role and wish their constructive energies to be applied for the university's good, but these worthies are usually a minority, are put on committees and sub-committees where their talents are diluted, and generally tradition and the institutional machine are too well-entrenched against them.

This edifice is supported by an elaborate and often ramshackle committee scaffolding; elaborate, because of the centrifugal advisory structures of universities allied to a participatory enthusiasm among staff; ramshackle, because it has seldom been overhauled, with new committees being piled on old ones, 'zero-basing' being not usually rampant in universities! The nature of the academic mind enhances the general impotence in decision-taking: trained to reason and argue logically rather than make up his mind by appeal to experience, pragmatism, expediency or flair, the academic reaches conclusions rather than makes decisions. When decisions *are* taken they tend to the parochial, a restriction of focus guaranteed by the university committee structure as much as by the cast of the members' minds. In universities, Northcote Parkinson's 'laws of committees' reach their full flower. Even if action is agreed there are no executives to implement it or managers to organise it, only administrators who as often as not simply 'administer' its reference to another committee. Add to all this the permanent tenure of most established academic staff, secure even against

94

redundancy, and the corporate manager's nightmare is complete.

The university machine is devised to allow staff to teach, research, debate and publish—which after all is what they are employed to do—without let or hindrance except the law of the land and their statutory requirements not to offend the religious creeds of their students and to avoid various types of 'disgraceful behaviour', usually indulgently defined. In particular, they are free to teach and to express the most hostile and heterodox views immune from sanction from governments, power blocs, or even their own employers. Staff defend this structure and point to the evils that can befall society where their freedom is compromised or destroyed: it is no accident that intolerant regimes try to control or politicise the university system, or even close it. In Nkrumah's Ghana and Idi Amin's Uganda, to name but two, each dictator made himself chancellor of the university and interfered massively in its academic affairs, then closed it. Liberal-minded laity also defend the structure which their influence (through the Privy Council in the UK, for example, who must approve university charters) had largely created: the checks and balances in the modern university corpus of statutes, the product of long evolutionary years of this liberal tradition, are indeed beautiful to behold. Academic freedom, permanent tenure, the placing of the individual above the corporation, may have a self-indulgent, spurious, even a farcical side, but many see it as an important if expensive and 'inefficient' corner-stone in the edifice of our civilisation. Indeed, as the custodians of absolute and timeless values, little in university *constitutions* has changed fundamentally since Newman's deathless Dublin lectures[1]—comparison of the statutes of the newest in the UK or Ireland, the University of Ulster, with older ones shows merely changes in focus and emphasis. No one has bettered the words of Thomas Hobbes over 300 years ago:

For, seeing the Universities are the fountains of civil and moral doctrine, from whence the preachers and the gentry, draining such water as they find, use to sprinkle the same upon the people, there ought certainly to be great care taken to have it pure both from the venom of heathen politicians and from the incantation of deceiving spirits.[2]

Such a structure is clearly ill-suited to the needs and imperatives of commerce; try its underlying philosophy on any businessman, investment analyst, the Securities and Exchange Commission in USA or the Securities and Investment Board in UK for example. No business would tolerate a board of directors which did not direct, which had many external nominees and employee representatives, and which exercised control over only half the firm's affairs. No business could run without executives and managers, on-line command, corporate objectives, strategic and financial plans, targetted achievement and performance indicators, alertness to market positioning, and the other *desiderata* of the commercial concern. Business favours strong executives; universities ensure weak ones or none at all. Business centralises policy-making and executes it through strong on-line management; universities do just the opposite. Universities have virtually no defined performance indicators, staff targets, 'fitness' records, personnel assessments, market reviews of products, or after-sales service. To be fair, universities are changing rapidly in these areas without subverting their constitutions—in the UK under the influence of the Jarratt Report,[3] stimulated by the ethos of the present government, most particularly its doctrinaire opposition to permanent tenure for academic staff which they are soon to end by legislation. To be fair also, the bulk of university income is from an annual parliamentary (or Dáil) vote of public money specifically to finance teaching and research, *not* for other purposes, especially not as risk capital. The question is: is the human product or active component of such a system equally ill-suited to the business world? The academic and business worlds and most of their inhabitants will always differ in motivation, expectation, priorities, time scales, and criteria and perceptions of success. The culture shock of entering the other's world is severe, though happily not irreversible. Yet academics are often employed by business, sometimes with high success, and I turn now to consider why this should be and how they can best be employed.

THE ACADEMIC IN BUSINESS

The involvement in commerce of university staff *as individuals* is not new but is as old as universities themselves. Members of medieval faculties took private fees (the good ones take plenty of them), most of which admittedly were earned through tutoring but also through professional practice and consultancy. University 'assured' stipends were modest, much indeed was payment in kind, and were bolstered by class fees of attending students, a form of performance-linked income. But externally-derived income was *ad hoc* and confined to those with marketable skills: in the older faculties, those in medicine and the law; in the newer, nineteenth-century ones, those in agriculture, chemistry, engineering, geology, and the like. To recognise and facilitate these differences some university chairs were until recently part-time. In Queen's University, Belfast, for example, chairs in clinical medical subjects, law, public health, biochemistry, and geology, carried the lowest remuneration until World War II.

The main industrial model of collaboration was, put simply, the tapping by commercial concerns of the knowledge and professional expertise of university staff who had something profitable to sell; the sole type of arrangement was the commercial contract: in this, industry, as the customer, says what it wants; the member of staff does it if he can; and the customer pays, often indeed very little, since an indulgent university rarely costed out the product, absorbed many overheads, and undercharged for intellectual rights—that is, of course, when the university was even aware of the staff's involvement. Only in recent years have central guidelines on economic costing (in UK, from the University Grants Committee) been issued. This amateur (my academic colleagues would prefer altruistic!) approach combined with the traditional aloofness of university scholars to science and applied sciences, and a robust anti-intellectualism in the business community (not to mention in parliament and even government), was a deadly brew which had much to do with the failure of Britain during 'the second industrial revolution' in the post-steam era, and cannot be absolved from blame for a disappointing performance in the contemporary 'third industrial revolution'.

Primitive state corporatism in Europe did rather better in creating *Technische Hochschules, polytechniques,* and the like, at a time when most scientific progress in Britain was made *not* in universities but in endowed research institutes, some industry, and by independent scholars of private-means, as a roll-call of Britain's scientific and industrial innovators clearly shows. These, the social stratifications, and the stigmata of trade, science, and commerce in especially England, meant that there was little *commitment* by the class-conscious university of the time to any form of involvement in business beyond that of individuals on a contract basis. Neither were boardrooms any place for academics *qua* academics, and large swathes of industry were controlled by small numbers of stock-holders, frequently family aggregated, who were often ill-equipped for the task and who measured their own success in terms of an acquired rural estate and resultant status rather than in their company accounts.

The modern academic involved in business at boardroom level therefore comes to his new task from an environment of vastly different perceptions and imperatives, from an institution historically uninvolved in, and even in some of its darker recesses hostile to, industry and commerce, and has a mind trained on lines and for purposes remote from those of business. He can, however, bring to business certain useful abilities which may be summarised as follows.

First, as has been well said, dons may be difficult but most are clever. Their intellectual discipline and ability allow them to grasp complex arguments and perceive their strengths and weaknesses. They have well-trained memories and forensic skills, and many have excellent and dispassionate reasoning powers. Some have in time become executives, others are entrepreneurs *manqué* and the business environment has released their skills. Even if few have emulated Professor Erhardt, the author of the post-war German *Wirtschafts-wunder*, and other ex-academic corporate leaders in UK and especially in USA, many have much to contribute. *Second*, they bring to the boardroom the intellectual facets of their training, thus extending the arena of debate. *Third*, as the product of a centrifugal and non-centralist configuration with regard to power structure, they are unlikely to have many in-hibitions in honestly and forthrightly expressing their views: few successful career academics have a reputation for reti-cence. *Fourth*, they provide at high level a window or conduit into the academic world which should increasingly be to the advantage of business—who benefit from contact with educational institutions on all fronts, from research con-tracts to staff training and recruitment—and reciprocally to the advantage of the academic world. *Fifth*, as a legacy of history their worlds and those of business only marginally overlap and so they bring fresh knowledge and contacts to the boardroom. *Sixth,* most have some special skill, some professional knowledge, which may help the board or management by way of *technical* advice or opinion—in economics, agriculture, accountancy, the law, engineering, business management, etc., although in my own speciality (medicine) opportunities are more limited and, fortunately, have not yet presented themselves! *Seventh*, their often naïve contributions to the board on business matters are a reminder to that board that the clientèle of the enterprise is also often naïve and that marketing and customer relationships have to take this into account. And *eighth*, honesty compels me to add that the academic's values and approach may appear to the commercially minded so bizarre that the executives take new heart in the wisdom of their own vocation.

THE BUSINESSMAN IN ACADEME

If the academic experiences a cultural shock in business, how much more does the businessman when exposed to the academic world? Not as much as many think. To begin with, many senior managers and board members have attended a higher education institution and (being clever) have often done well: at this early stage of their career they have been exposed to the tenets and practices of the intellectual. Many have a high regard for 'culture'—some through a genuine liking, others as a means of countering their commercial image—and incline to the belief that 'academic' and 'cultured' are synonymous, a flattering if incorrect assumption. Most have or had children in the higher education system. The titles 'Dr' and 'Professor' have, to them, real if often inflated connotations of status and respectability. Industrialists, in my experience, rate recognition from universities (chancellorships, pro-chancellorships, honorary degrees, etc.) very highly, more highly even than exalted office in their own professional body, which they take as no more than their due. Furthermore, in their own work they rely on the knowledge of specialists—accountants, lawyers and the like—who have benefited from tertiary education, while their high concern with manpower training and deployment leads them to value training and educative skills. Many businessmen, therefore, when dealing with the academic world are dealing with one of which they have knowledge and for which they have a high regard even if their understanding is incomplete and some of their more commercial instincts alien to it. It is when they move from being a beneficiary, direct or indirect, to becoming involved in university government (universities have 'governing bodies'. not boards of directors), or dealing closely with the university machine in some other way, that disenchantment begins. I have already said enough to indicate broadly why: how then can the businessman stimulate enterprise and help in the governance of universities?

I believe he can do so in two ways. *First*, as a member of the governing body he will have a role at the highest decision-taking and policy-making level. He should use this position to help the university in those corporate aspects of its affairs which are of increasing importance and which have lain for too long neglected—strategic and financial planning; contingency positioning; cost-effective measurement; staff deployment and training; and above all in persuading the academics that *every* institution requires clear objectives, aims and goals, a consensus on a 'plan' as to how these may be achieved, the command structure to ensure that the policies are efficiently and effectively implemented, and a review procedure on corporate and divisional progress and control management—persuading them, too, of the fact that 'accountability' is not a dirty 14-letter word but the key to any form of effective institutional activity.

This is routine to the adept businessman; what requires skill of a high order is to convince the students and academics that this philosophy in no way strikes at 'academic freedom' or subverts the university charter, still less is it planned to introduce wholesale the ethics of the market economy to seats of learning, but that it will actually release resources and guarantee a more efficient organisation in which academics' careers and activities can flourish. It will require perception and self-discipline for a businessman to constrain his enthusiasms and activities to the matters outlined above and in no way crudely insinuate his views into matters very properly the preserve of the academic body—curricula, student affairs, academic standards, research and the like—and, most difficult of all, to recognise how strongly and sincerely academics see themselves as custodians of something absolute, true, and beautiful—scholarship—which they consider to be currently under threat and at all costs to be preserved from Hobbes's 'the venom of heathen politicians and from the incantation of deceiving spirits'. And the businessman must work within a structure seemingly ill-suited for the task though he will soon see that most university constitutions are flexible to the point of licence and will allow nearly anything.

In my view all this can best be done through activity on certain key committees, working groups and the rest, particularly in finance, development and investment. Confining his involvement to constantly voting against or seeking to amend recommendations of these bodies in the decision-making council will only entrench staff in their belief that businessmen are incorrigible and perfidious and, as a result, such action will be divisive and ultimately unsuccessful. In short, he should not try to make universities like businesses but rather to introduce to universities good general management practices. If he does this he will be a paragon indeed. This is a more ambitious and active mission than that of the academic in business, to which I will return later.

Second, he can play a crucial role in certain new university/commerce developments. Since it is impossible to make universities like businesses, and since they hang today somewhere between what Geoffrey Price has called 'the corporate state and the market', their ultimate position as yet uncertain, and since no business wishes to bankrupt itself by adopting university structures, there is no real alternative but to devise a new collaborative corporate structure which can market the university's products and fully use its assets yet not subvert its primary purposes in advancing and imparting knowledge. If we cannot turn a frog into a prince or a prince into a frog, let us try to produce from them something that will look good and can jump as well! The individually negotiated commercial contract is outdated as the sole mechanism of collaboration. Recently, under the whip of financial necessity, government pressure and the rhetoric of 'UK plc', and helped by more commercially-minded vice-chancellors, some universities have made a virtue of constructing such arrangements—science parks, CAMPUS (Salford University), AURIS (Aberdeen University), and others, most building on pre-existing though modest industrial liaison arrangements. Queen's was in the van and in 1983 formed QUBIS (Queen's University Business and Information Service) with its market-orientated wholly university-owned subsidary QUBIS Ltd. (in 1984), a limited liability company registered under the company acts with articles of association, a board of directors, a company secretary, a managing director, a chairman, and an authorised share capital of £500,000 with £100,000 issued and taken up by the university using its private (not public) money. It is wholly and unequivocally in the commercial world: its aim is to market the skills of staff members to industry and commerce, identify commercially exploitable research and pull it through to the market, and it is empowered to establish subsidiary companies, for

103

example to develop university property or to participate in equity sharing joint ventures. It is as a main board member, or on the board of one of these joint ventures, that I believe the businessman on the university governing body can be of great help since he can deploy his expertise and use his contacts and acumen in an environment in which he is most at home and free from the tortuous committee structure and constitutional constraints of the mainline university.

THE NON-EXECUTIVE DIRECTOR

Much has been written about the function and role of the non-executive director in a large public company: his relationships with the executives, how far he should intrude in management decisions and actions, and how he should deploy his skills and the information he may have from other boardrooms. Who does he represent in the narrower sense—shareholders, staff, customers, etc, or in the wider sense of society, the public interest, and the commercial conscience? What special rights should he be given, e.g. in electing or otherwise the chairman (as in the Guinness affair), and should he trade in or even hold the company's stock? Some even take a more basic view—why have non-executive directors at all?

These issues invite instructive and lively debate, beyond the scope of this essay: the distillation of my views is that there should be non-executive directors to introduce a balance and a perspective to the views and opinions of management, to prevent an executive-only board which tends to become xenophobic and too closely identified with the management whom in their *alter-ego* they in fact are, and to widen the contacts, understanding, and conceptual appreciation of the board and portray the company to a wide public in the best and most proper light.

As the Promotion of Non-Executive Directors (UK), a

body set up by the Bank of England and a group of City Institutions has put it: 'non-executive directors can provide the board with knowledge, expertise, judgement and balance which may not be available if the board consists only of full-time executives'.[4] The non-executive director should be committed to do his best for the company, give the board his full support and loyalty, follow scrupulously the company guidelines on behaviour and practice, have a prime regard for the standing in society as well as the financial performance of the company, have no part in anything which offends his ethics or principles, and be prepared to resign if he is no longer of value to the company or if he finds himself at serious odds on fundamentals with the majority of his non-executive colleagues. In strict theory he should probably not own any of the company's stock and so maintain his complete independence, but in practice this is usually seen as lack of commitment and moreover an unnecessary *cordon sanitaire* for a person with the rectitude appropriate to a non-executive director. A modest stock holding makes an acceptable compromise. Stock options and the like are a different matter and most public companies which operate such schemes wisely restrict them to executives. The non-executive director should always voice his views inside the boardroom: indeed since he is independent he has a duty and a freedom to press points which his executive colleagues for various reasons may hesitate to do.

The Code of Conduct of a large Irish public company embodies the above views when, in essence, its 18 pages and 15-page Appendix crystallises as the following: 'That subject to his giving his primary commitment to his primary business or professional involvement, he (or she) should give priority to the interests of the company and avoid activities discreditable to him or her or the board or embarrassing to the company ...'.

All this is clear enough; what is more problematical is:

105

(a) how can be best serve the company if he has little expertise in the business; (b) to what extent should he be involved in policy-making other than in the formal sense of having a voice and vote at the board e.g. should he be actively involved in policy formulation at committees of earlier reference either independently, jointly with executive directors or with management. In a pragmatic sense the first of these (a) is simple and I have addressed it above, though philosophically it is more difficult. But (b) presents more difficulty since the practice of businessmen in Academe differs from that of academics in business; it is this latter that I will now briefly discuss.

The increasing size and complexity of business make the role of the non-executive director ever more important. The regulatory bodies see and encourage a greater role for non-executive directors not just in the boardrooms but on certain committees of which so-called 'Audit Committees' serve as perhaps the best example. Such committees are not required by law but for at least the last ten years the accountancy bodies and their Auditing Practices Committee have been arguing for them with government. Thus they have come to be regarded not just as a means of better financial control and overview but also as a means of strengthening the influence of non-executive directors and auditors, which is considered in modern conditions to be wholly desirable. In fact non-executive directorships for those of the requisite quality is becoming something of a growth industry! A private member's bill (UK) of 1983 which sought to legislate for the minimum number of non-executive directors in companies of varying sizes failed because there were too few persons judged as qualified so to act; since then board rooms have seemingly recruited energetically and the standards proposed in 1983 had by 1985 been nearly met. Catching up was certainly overdue: the New York Stock Exchange stipulates that an Audit Committee should be made up solely of 'directors independent of management and free from any relationship that, in the opinion of the board of directors, would interfere with the exercise of independent judgement as a committee member', i.e. non-executive directors. They are also held at law responsible for reviewing the results of audits and the company's code of conduct, and they have an overview of the activities of the company's officers.

Corporate events in London during 1986-7 can only have fuelled the non-executive director growth industry since increasing attention is being focused on a board of directors' statutory and common law responsibilities to shareholders and its duties to employees, customers and (in the case of a bank) depositors, and the fiduciary duty of directors to act in the interests of the company, and at all times to exercise care and skill, to observe the utmost good faith towards the company, and to act honestly in the exercise of their powers. Audit committees and the overview by non-executive directors are widely seen as an important development in ensuring probity in management and upholding share-holders', employees' and customers' rights. As recently as January 1987 the Banking Supervision Division of the Bank of England was issuing guidelines whose central thrust was along the above lines.[5]

But if, as regulatory bodies see it, the principal role of non-executive directors is to take an objective view of the policies and views advanced by management, how can such directors act with executives and managers in jointly formulating policy for consideration by the board? The answer is — not easily, if at all. This also suits management who see it as their own role to bring forward policies to the board for decision or assessment in the scale of priorities, unencumbered by formal contributions by the board (except as articulated in policy guidelines). In short: non-executive directors are expected to contribute at the board, to inform themselves and be informed, to be active on audit committees (where they should be in a large majority) and in nomination committees, sponsoring committees and the like, but not to be involved formally at sub-board level with policy formulation or management matters. Such delineation will of course be tempered in practice and influenced by whether or not the board chairman is executive or non-executive.

At first sight this is very different to the highly participatory role I outlined for the businessman in the university structure, especially at 'sub-governing body' level. On closer examination the difference narrows. If the central function of a university—advancing and imparting knowledge, and awarding degrees (academic assessment)—is equated with that of a business—making and marketing goods—then the roles of the businessman (on the university governing body) and the non-executive director (on the board) are very similar: in fact the former is *less* not more participatory. But in the *management of the institution and support structures and policy relating to them* the former has more scope and can do his best work by participating more, as I have set out above. This was enunciated in 1985 in very practical terms by a committee in UK chaired by the industrialist, Sir Alex Jarratt.[6] The proposals go far though they stop short of academic interference except by contingent change: academic matters were explicitly excluded from Jarratt's brief. Jarratt's proposals were unashamedly corporate in their model: the university governing body should act like a board of directors; the vice-chancellor should be called 'chief executive' and act like one; strategic plans should be laid with the involvement of lay members; and rolling financial programmes, critical success factors, identification of markets, plans for targeting, frequent 'positioning' assessments, monitoring of progress, and the rest of the corporate package should all be activated; and there should be accountability, on-line management, an end to permanent tenure for academic staff, performance indicators, and much else besides. UK universities were enjoined to implement his recommendations or take the consequences; all have taken the first option. Sir Alex himself has a personal 'mission statement', to make sure they do what he says by travelling the country explaining how his ideas do not endanger basic academic tenets. The report was not an isolated one, it has its counterpart in Griffith's Report advising more management efficiency in the National Health Service.[7] I think Sir Alex is correct, and undoubtedly there is both scope and need for a businessman's attitudes and skills in universities to help the university develop its business enterprise and to run its corporate self better. If so, I hope businessmen may agree with and even learn something from this essay, and if academics learn something also, it will be a welcome bonus.

EPILOGUE

There are more basic aspects of business culture which many academics find alien, namely the whole idea of the corporate ethos and the profit motive, even capitalism itself. It is no accident that the intellectual leaders of such radicalism are mostly found among the international academic community, in the United States almost exclusively so. The very size of the corporate sector, the growth of the multinationals, and the great power and influence big business wields in shaping our economic and social life and fashioning our culture, make it inevitable that some non-executive directors (and not only those from an academic background) wish to broaden the boardroom agenda to include the social implications of business policy. To them, America may be larger than General Motors. They may even believe that business policy should be tempered by its social implications. (More radical citizens would have the former *determined* by the latter, but they would not normally be found in boardrooms!). This intriguing topic is a subject in itself but my essay would be incomplete without some references to the problem which I confine to this epilogue as being beyond the essay's scope.

The wider agenda visualised should be a concern of the non-executive director who, though pledged to the articles of association, perforce works on a broader canvas than the executive. In a sense his constituency is society. He should ensure that the general consequences of corporate action are consistently before the board. He should remember that industry in general has a bad track record in this field, and that failure of 'enlightened self-interest' and its replacement by legislation or state corporation for the public good is a basic theme of our social history. Most public companies recognise their philanthropic duty which they discharge in support for education, health, the arts, community services, and good works generally, often earmarking a predetermined percentage of their profits for the purpose. Some megarich industrialists have created philanthropic foundations—Ford, Rockefeller, Nuffield, among others. No matter that some fund-giving inevitably has a promotional and advertising spin-off, the causes benefit. All public companies undertake or sponsor market research into the acceptability of their products and how this may be improved with the object of enhancing sales and profits. But is this enough? Should not business sponsor research into the consequences of its activities for society at large, a more daring and radical concept which goes beyond the narrower world of their activities as 'price-administering oligopolists'.[8] I believe it should as a duty. It is morally wrong to market a product aggressively without knowing its effect on society; at present this is limited to physical and toxicological effects, but there are many others. More narrowly it can be in the business's commercial interests to carry out such research. The dilemma involved is illustrated by the tobacco industry whose products have wide social and economic as well as health consequences and whose ambitious research activities have helped to develop more acceptable and easily marketable products less detrimental to the health of the persistent smoker, and in consequence have countered the strong downward market for its main product (cigarettes) and minimised government intervention. This facet of commerce is a topic for boardroom initiative by non-executive directors, a new dimension to business 'enterprise', but one now jostling to the front of the queue. It should not be left to consumer groups to appear to force recognition from a grudging board; the board should be initiator or partner.

RICHARD KEARNEY

5. *Postmodern Ireland*

IRELAND is undergoing an ideological crisis. The inherited models of identity which provided people on this island with a sense of belonging and direction appear to be losing their authority. And nothing new has emerged to replace them. Ireland, it could be said, is now devoid of any guiding ideology. So what is to be done? The first thing, I would suggest, is to face up to the crucial implications of this ideological decline; and the second is to try to outline a project for the future. What kind of ideas might positively motivate Irish men and women as we face into the nineteen nineties? That is my question.

Our famous, or infamous, 'identity crisis' may well prove to be one of our greatest assets. Whereas other Western nations—such as France, Britain, America—assume a stable and unquestioned identity, we in Ireland today at least know that we do not know who exactly we are or where exactly we are going to. In the fall-out of the protracted violence in Northern Ireland, we can harbour no illusions about the 'destiny of the nation'. Moreover, as a political commentator recently remarked, one of the advantages of living in a peripheral and highly visible country like Ireland is that 'national myths and self-images are always kept well above the threshold of one's awareness'.[1] The English or French citizen subconsciously regards his/her myths as universal and self-evident. The American inhabits a vast continent where matters of national purpose and stability are taken for granted. But the Irish person is uneasily aware that his/her set of ideological assumptions are always subject to question. This situation has the virtue—for the cultural critic at least—of allowing political viewpoints to find an unusually clear and often self-conscious expression. Irish nationalists (unlike French, English or American nationalists) know that they are nationalists. And the same generally goes for Irish Unionists. In consequence, 'political philosophies which elsewhere hide behind liberal, conservative or radical generalities tend to parade naked in public in Ireland'.[2] Similarily, when a particular political ideology breaks down, it does so for all to see.

I

Ideologies are generally based on some foundational story or myth which a community relates to itself or to others in order to explain its identity. The established ideologies of Ireland, north and south, no longer seem adequate to the needs of its citizens. The nationalist ideology of a united Ireland—based on the narratives of 1916, the Fenian risings and heroic memories of martyrdom — has ceased to mobilise a dynamic sense of 'national' consensus. The unionist ideology of unconditional loyalty to the British Crown—based on narratives of siege, resistance and divine election (as commemorated in the ritual insignia of the Orange Lodges or the Apprentice Boys Parade)—is now largely redundant in the face of the present situation in Northern Ireland. Although the rhetoric survives, it ceases to fit reality. As models of ideological bonding, nationalism and unionism have become increasingly anachronistic. And yet no alternative has been found to fill the gap. The nation-states live on, but in the guise of a centralised bureaucracy which has become too anonymous and distant from its citizens to elicit any sense of genuine allegiance.

I want to consider here some of the implications of this

break-up of the traditional ideologies. The solution to the crisis is not to be found, I believe, in the modern cult of consumerist individualism (everyone for him/herself), but rather in a *postmodern* model of society. Such a postmodern model would seek to transcend both the traditional postures of the nation-state and the modern retreat into individualism. It would involve, as I will be suggesting, a radical pluralism and regionalism, bringing power and decision-making to a level that people can identify with.

Our discussion here is not being conducted in terms of empirical social science or political economy. We are dealing less with the 'facts' than with the framework of cultural concepts in which the 'facts' are interpreted and evaluated. Of course, the ideological crisis in Irish society which specifically concerns us reflects, in a dialectical manner, a breakdown of social life. The cogency or weakness of communal images, myths and narratives are always in some way related to developments in the everyday infrastructure of society. Consequently, when I use cultural-ideological concepts such as 'tradition', 'modernity' and 'post-modernity', I do so in the conviction that they are sensitive barometers of changes taking place in the most basic spheres of social life. More exactly, the postmodern paradigm of radical pluralism I am proposing is one which, I believe, responds and corresponds to actual and potential developments within Irish society today. The postmodern project is not some abstract fantasy to be imposed on reality. It is, rather, an attempt to make a virtue of necessity by re-thinking in a positive way the contemporary state of affairs—i.e. the fragmentation of traditional ideologies, the break-up of the nation-state, the failure of centralised government, the social and cultural alienation of modern individualism, and the rise of a global communications network. The postmodern option of a radical pluralism seeks

114

to go beyond the present and co-existing extremes of (a) a centralised state bureaucracy and (b) a medley of private individuals devoid of any communal project.[3]

A national ideology begins to degenerate into rhetoric when it ceases to address the reality of people's experience. To take a topical example, what positive relevance have the old revivalist ideologies of Irish nationalism (or unionism) to the citizens of Jobstown, a new housing development in Dublin, where over 60 per cent are unemployed, less than 14 per cent church goers, alarmingly low numbers turn out at national elections and high rates of truancy and vandalism exist amongst the young? However noble the ideology of a Gaelic, Catholic, nationalist culture, and however justly cherished by the founding fathers and established political parties of the Republic, it is no longer adequate to the needs and aspirations of such an urbanised and uprooted population. While the traditional national ideology may still serve an important ceremonial and commemorative purpose, it is no longer motivating the majority of Irish citizens in a creative way. A yawning gap has emerged between the official expressions of the nation-state and the everyday experience of its citizens. As David Stevens of the Irish Council of Churches recently observed: 'There is a crisis in our traditional ideologies—both religious and political—at the moment'.[4] It is in this context that an alternative post-modern model of radical pluralism is advocated. But this does not require that we jettison our rich cultural heritage. It means that we *reinterpret* it in a manner more adequate to the challenge of the present.

II

The relevance of such a postmodern model is not confined to Ireland. The nation-state is also breaking up elsewhere—in neighbouring countries like Britain and France no less than here in Ireland. But we are, arguably, one of the most explicit examples of this fragmentation: a sort of litmus test of things to come elsewhere. The fissures and divisions are especially conspicuous here since Irish society has been commonly regarded as a cohesive and homogeneous entity. And so the dramatic fracturing of this society—due to pressures of post-colonial uncertainty, partition, economic fragility and, most crucially, the recent bloody conflicts in Northern Ireland—has captured international attention. It is, perhaps, because the process of ideological bonding has been so strong in Ireland that its recent breakdown has received such a high profile.

But the British and French nations are also experiencing inner disruption. Britain is divided between the affluent Tory south and the deprived Labour north as well as between indigenous and immigrant populations. France is still divided between the Parisian centre and regional peripheries, while there is a growing recognition that France—like Britain, Germany and many other European nations—is fast developing into a multi-ethnic, multi-linguistic, multi-cultural society. The European nation-states have generally camouflaged their inner fragmentation and diversification by opting for strong national leaders (e.g. Thatcher, Mitterand) whose univocal authority on the domestic and international stage preserves a veneer of unity. But the *una-voce—uno-duce* strategy is only a holding operation.

Europe will soon follow Ireland down the path of ideological crisis. And this is why Ireland might well serve as a pilot-model for its European neighbours. It can only do so, of course, if it succeeds in resolving its present dilemma, projecting a viable postmodern alternative to the prevailing ideology of the centralised nation-state with its corollary of atomic individualism. Viewed from such a perspective, Ireland's difficulty may be seen as Europe's opportunity (as well as Ireland's own). Ireland's postmodern project might well serve as a vanguard movement for the wider world.

III

The postmodern project seeks to transcend the confines of insular nationalism. But this does not mean denying that certain forms of nationalism have often served, historically, as legitimate ideologies of resistance and emancipation. In our own century, one could cite the nationalist opposition to US imperialism in Vietnam and Nicaragua, and to Soviet Imperialism in Hungary, Czechslovakia, Poland or Afghanistan. Not to mention the struggle of European nations against Nazi occupation in the Second World War or the campaigns waged by African nations against the colonial policies of white supremacy. One might also note here that the history of Irish nationalism has itself been a relatively noble one—with the obvious exception of the Provisional IRA's campaign of sectarian slaughter (and the corresponding Loyalist campaign). What is certain is that one must *discriminate* between different kinds of political nationalism—those that emancipate and those that incarcerate, those that nourish and those that oppress, those that affirm a people's cultural identity in dialogue with other peoples and those that degenerate into ideological closure—into xenophobia, racism and bigotry.

However, to go beyond nationalism—in its insular and hegemonic guises—is not to succumb to the opposite extreme of anti-nationalism. Gut anti-nationalism—as we know so well in the Irish context—is quite as blind as gut nationalism. And it can be even more intellectually represensible in so far as it presumes to be on the side of the angels. The Irish nationalist is generally prepared to admit his/her ideological credentials. But this is not always the case with anti-nationalists. Often, those who crudely equate *all* forms of nationalism with reactionary and irridentist fanaticism do so in the name of some neutral or transcendental standpoint which in fact *masks* their own (unacknowledged) ideological bias. To roundly condemn Irish nationalism, refusing to distinguish between its constitutional and non-constitutional expressions, *without* also adverting to the historical sins of British colonialism and unionism, amounts to a tacit *apologia* of the latter.

But even if the nationalist ideology were to be superseded in a postmodern Ireland of the nineties, it could no doubt continue to play a valid role in our cultural and historical memory—as well as in related areas like indigenous music, dialects, crafts and sports. (Would any Irishman want to disown cyclists like Roche and Kelly or footballers like Best, Brady or Willie John McBride?) When we advocate a movement *beyond nationalism*, we do so with specific reference to the 'ideological' debate about the future identity of our society in a postmodern age. We do not for a moment deny that nationalism has played a legitimate and often enabling part in the historical shaping of Ireland. What we are advancing is the desirability of a transition from traditional nationalism to a post-nationalism which would endeavour to preserve all that is rich and valuable in the cultural memory of nationalism (and unionism) while opening onto more inclusive horizons of interaction.[5] Post-nationalism is not Pol-Potism: it recommends a creative reinterpretation of the past, not its liquidation.

To be post-nationalist is also to be trans-nationalist. It is to transcend borders. This should not be confused with multi-nationalism. If the solution to our present crisis does not lie in the revivalist dream of a unified 'nation once again', nor in a blanket dismissal of all that nationalism has achieved, neither does it lie in the gold rush of consumer multi-nationalism. Selling oneself out to the highest financial bidder or compromising one's freedom in some geo-political power block, West or East, offers no answer.

Orwell's satiric depiction of Oceania in *1984* serves as a reminder of the dangers of such global anonymity. What we are arguing here is that beyond the alternatives of nationalist *independence* and multi-nationalist *dependence* there lies a third possibility—that of a trans-nationalist *inter-dependence*.

The undesirability of dependence on military-industrial power centres is obvious enough. This is particularly so for a society like ours whose sovereignty and neutrality have only been recently acquired. Less obvious perhaps are the dangers of nationalist independence. The claim to an autonomous national identity has been somewhat taken for granted in modern Irish history. But such a claim can sometimes degenerate into a protectionist or sectarian ideology which exalts one particular community to the detriment of others—particularly when they are minorities. The price of such ideological exclusiveness can be, at times, tribal intoler-ance on the home front and closure on the foreign front—that is, hostility to all cultures and societies of an 'alien' cast. And curiously, this form of insular nationalism (republican or loyalist) frequently goes hand in hand with a growing sense of individualism at a personal level (i.e. a denial of how one is always interconnected with others). Closing ourselves off from the outside world, we have in-creasingly resorted to the strategy of every man for himself. In this respect, Irish individualism may be seen as Irish nationalism writ small. 'Ourselves alone' corresponds to 'the self alone'.

The cultural crisis of modern Ireland stems, in part at least, from the schizophrenic co-existence of these twin expressions of negative independence. We have been pro-claiming ourselves a 'race apart' in matters of religion, morality and tradition while, as individuals, we have feathered our private nests—when given the oppor-tunity—with the economic handouts of modern

119

consumerism. We have been preaching one set of laws for the nation—as witnessed in our legislation on divorce and contraception for example—but practising quite another set of laws as individuals.

Tocqueville identified the modern drift towards individualism as the 'feeling which disposes each citizen to isolate himself from the mass of his fellows and withdraw into the circle of family and friends; with this little society formed to his taste, he gladly leaves the greater society to look after itself.... Such folk owe no man anything and hardly expect anything from anybody. They form the habit of thinking of themselves in isolation and imagine that their whole destiny is in their hands.[6] While Ireland has managed to preserve a sense of community for which she is justly appreciated this has, in recent times, ceased to express itself in a dynamic or creative manner.

It can scarcely be denied that the abstract ideology of the nation-state has tended, in the Republic, towards a rhetorical republicanism in which fewer and fewer of our citizens actually believe. Mounting apathy and even cynicism in the electorate's attitude to centralised party politics has resulted in the growth of a new cult of consumerist individualism. While the world of politics has become more centralised and the world of personal existence more privatised, the in-between world of community action and interaction has been minimalised.

Traditionally, the Church contributed much to this role of community, particularly in the areas of education, social welfare, parish activities and public morality. But—with some exceptions—this religious contribution has tended to operate from the top down rather than serving as the expression of democratic community involvement. It might even be said that in the contemporary ideological crisis, the Irish churches have been more part of the problem than of the solution. In their ultimate resistance—despite the appeasing rhetoric—to real ecumenism and pluralism, they have given substance to the maxim that Ireland has too much religion and not enough Christianity. The fact that one still speaks more of the 'Catholic' and 'Protestant' communities in Ireland than of 'Christian' communities—and usually to connote sectarian or confessional conflict (in street riots north of the border or referenda debates south of it)—speaks for itself. Those Irish Church leaders who dismiss ecumenists as 'à la carte' Christians forget that Christ and his disciples were 'à la carte' Jews. They reinterpreted the Judaic testament of prophecy and law in a new way—remaining faithful, as they saw it, to the essential promise of that tradition. What are ecumenists doing today if not advocating a free dialogue between the different Christian Churches—a dialogue conducive to the toleration, and indeed cultivation, of a diverse range of scriptural interpretations? Christian ecumenists are the true allies of those Jewish talmudists who argued that there are several meanings to every line in the Bible. *Either* pluralism *or* fundamentalism—that is the real issue for Irish Christians today.

IV

The postmodern model proposes a movement beyond *both* the traditionalist project of National Revival *and* the modern project of consumer individualism. It seeks, in other words, to circumvent the locked antagonism between tradition and modernity. But what exactly does the term 'postmodern' mean? One of its most important features is the new attitude it opens on history. The very notion of evolving historical periods (e.g. tradition, modernity) following each other in some kind of necessary causal order is put into question. Hence, rather than construing history as a *continuity* (leading inexorably back to a lost paradise or forward to a guaranteed future), postmodernism views it as a *collage*. It thus resists the naïve belief in history as demonstrating inevitable progress or regress, and suggests that we draw from the old and the new in a creative and non-dogmatic way. The 'post' in postmodern refers not just to what comes *after* modernity. It signals *another way of seeing things*, one which transforms the linear model of historical time into a series of multiple perspectives. The idea of a millenarian state in which all cultural and political differences are subsumed and a single viewpoint imposed is resisted by the postmodern preference for multiplicity, for an open-ended process of differentiation, for diversity without premature synthesis.

The architect, Charles Jencks, has described the post-modern aesthetic as one of 'radical eclecticism'. By this he means that it rejects the idea of a dominant centre or totality. All tendencies towards cultural uniformity are resisted. As applied to architecture, for example, this entails the liberty to mix together styles drawn from a variety of cultural or historical periods (Egyptian, Graeco-Roman, Celtic, medieval, Renaissance, Baroque, late-modernist, high-tech, functionalist etc.). As applied to literature, it might be said to correspond to Roland Barthes' notion of 'multiple writing' where the cultural text is recognised as a pluri-dimensional space of open invention and reinvention. One of the goals of this 'radical eclecticism' is to rid us of the illusion of some all-englobing ideology in order to accommo-date cultural differences. But it is important to distinguish this kind of radical eclecticism from the 'weak' or 'con-servative' kind which tolerates multiplicity simply by default, by an absence of commitment or purpose. The challenge of an enabling postmodernism is to turn the 'weak eclecticism' which increasingly dominates our contemporary mass-media and consumer society into a 'radical eclecticism' (or what might be called a *creative pluralism*). It strives to transform the existing jumble of cultural fragments into a meaningful jigsaw design.

V

How might this postmodern aesthetic be related to Irish culture? A propos of Irish art we could cite many works that advance the cause of creative pluralism. In literature, there is Joyce's celebration in *Finnegans Wake* of a 'poly-gutteral' culture which blends together native traditions of myth and memory with a wide assortment of foreign narratives (e.g. Biblical, Greek, Chinese and so on). In this way, Irish culture is positively portrayed as a 'circumbendibus' of multiple aspects, an on-going process of free migration which traverses a plurality of other cultures before returning to itself enlarged and enriched. To be true to ourselves, as Joyce put it, is to be 'othered'. Our task, as he once wittily remarked, is to 'hibernicise Europe and Europeanise Ireland'.

Many other Irish artists have developed the postmodern aesthetic of migration. The option to blend the 'foreign' with the 'familiar'—to construe the question of cultural identity as a frontierless toing and froing between national and international perspectives—is evident, for instance, in Beckett's nomadic narrators, Banville's inquisitive scientists, Le Brocquy's multi-faceted heads or Ballagh's parodies of the great classical masters (Vermeer, Da Vinci, Velasquez etc). Moreover, the postmodern artist generally blurs the distinction between the idioms of so-called 'high art' and 'popular culture'. There is a basic recognition that the artist can no longer be viewed according to the romantic aesthetic as some solitary romantic genius set apart from the 'masses'. He now becomes a participant in a cultural polyphony which exceeds the confines of his private psyche. Thus Joyce spoke of the penman giving way to the postman, art as a privileged

123

means of written communication between two isolated subjects giving way to art as part of the emerging multi-communications network. Le Brocquy speaks of the influence of photography and cinema—i.e. media of mechanical reproduction—on the 'kinetic' quality of his own series of multiple heads. And Ballagh brings the post-modern aesthetic of radical eclecticism to the point where art and popular culture begin to parody each other. He juxta-poses themes drawn from Renaissance portraiture on the one hand with the new mass-media culture of comic strips and television on the other. The multi-media works of a new generation of Irish artists including Martin Folen, Elanna O Kelly and James Coleman confirm the rich potential of the postmodern aesthetic. And in the field of music one could cite the extraordinary success of U2, the Pogues, Paul Brady or Van Morrison who have mixed vernacular and inter-national idioms to great effect, or Enya whose inventive use of electronic synthesizers to blend popular Irish folk with motifs from other musical cultures has also won appreciation on a world scale. Finally, the impact of innovative Irish films like Neil Jordan's *Angel* or Pat Murphy's *Maeve* offer further evidence of how Irish culture is becoming increasingly enriched by its openness to other cultures—both in the sense of contributing to them and learning from them. Indeed, Pat Murphy has made the point that genuine inter-nationalism—in contrast to trendy mid-Atlantic oppor-tunism—is *complementary* to cultural regionalism. The necessity to develop an Irish film culture is, she argues accordingly, 'not out of any self-obsessed navel-gazing, but because what is most specifically local is also most relevant internationally'.[7]

To switch our attention to a more microcosmic level of cultural activity, we might note how a new spate of journals in Ireland seems to be anticipating the postmodern turn towards intercultural exchange and regional pluralism. *The Crane Bag* was, from its inception in 1977, committed to the cultivation of cultural differences. As the opening editorial stated: 'The critical disposition of *The Crane Bag* cannot provide a fixed or total perspective. Precisely because it is never complete, its borders always shifting, disintegrating, reforming, it is a reminder that we are history's creation and history ours'. More recent journals have developed this commitment to cultural pluralism. The second editorial of *Graph* (1987) tells us that 'reinvention comes through exchange not imitation' and that its brief is to 'stress the nature of links which go both ways, inwards and outwards'. Striking a similar note, two cultural journals from the West of Ireland, *Krino* and *Salmon*, have argued for the importance of 'regional centres of literary activity which are not provincial but look outward'. And *Riverline*, emanating from Waterford, affirms the need for a cultural 'outlet from the South East' while simultaneously insisting that literature 'knows no borders or boundaries'. Finally, the editor of the new critical forum in the *Honest Ulsterman* adds his voice to the project of cultural pluralism when he speaks of going beyond 'unitary thinking that has so far leap-frogged the differences which are reality in Ireland'. And he adds elsewhere: 'The unitary ideologies of nationalism and post-partition unionism are apparently in collapse and we seem to be in a post-nationalist, post-unionist transition . .' (*Irish Review*, 4). These and other pleas for a new cultural pluralism are perhaps telling, if discrete, signals of a post-modern Ireland in the making—one where regionalism would avoid the pitfall of provincialism and where pluralism would avoid the anaemic condition of 'weak eclecticism'.[8]

VI

Rather than viewing the postmodern scenario of cultural

eclecticism with alarm, we might be better advised therefore to try to turn it to our advantage. For example, might not a very simple fact like our geographical status as a maritime island be considered (as our history reminds us) as an occasion for mobility, circulation and exploration rather than for isolation?[9] Similarly, could not our location on the periphery of Europe between North America and Britain be positively exploited in the context of the new communications culture? Instead of seeing ourselves as permanently dwarfed by the power-blocs of East and West, could we not be using the available communications technology to export our culture to others as well as to import it from others? A real opportunity for this is soon to be available through the European Space Agency Satellites which from 1989 will offer facilities for Education centres in Ireland to link up free of charge with their counterparts around Europe. Availing of our privileged access to the major First World information centres, could we not be simultaneously establishing contact with other small and post-colonial societies in the Second and Third Worlds? Our voting record in the United Nations on issues such as South Africa, Nuclear Disarmament and Central America—in addition to Frank Aiken's influential sponsorship of the Nuclear Non-Proliferation Treaty in the fifties—are indicators, at a political level, of how Ireland's role as a mediating link between the privileged and under-privileged parts of the world can be deployed in a constructive fashion.

This radical potential for international mediation has yet to be realised in the specific realm of communications. But the possibilities are all there. Indeed the 1984 UNESCO report on a New World Communications Order made some interesting suggestions as to how smaller peripheral societies might work to decentralise and democratise the existing global information system. Ireland's contribution to such a decentralising process could be significant. As a distinct island geographically situated within the British Isles, as a non-NATO member of the EEC, as a transatlantic stepping stone to North America, our dual insider-outsider status could become our greatest asset in the context of international relations and communications. Bob Geldof's Live Aid phenomenon has shown us how the satellite media provide new possibilities for global intercommunication and interdependence: possibilities which can actively benefit dispossessed and underprivileged peoples. This promise of a global community of communities, radically decentralised and radically interrelated, is one of the most challenging prospects of a postmodern communications culture.

Postmodern culture crosses national boundaries. It is culture without frontiers. But in order to resist the domination of a centralised bureaucracy of communication, the postmodern task is to ensure that a culture without frontiers does not degenerate into a culture without differences. In order to safeguard the radical decentralisation of the communications resources, it is important to ensure that it is not only the media of *production* (video, radio, film, print) that are made democratically available and accountable but also the entire system of *distribution*.[10] There is no point in having a cinema in every street or a video in every house if they are all showing the same film. There is no point in having thirty cable channels if twenty of them are broadcasting 'Charley's Angels'—who, in turn, differ only in the colour of their hair.

VII

Postmodernism, as mentioned, represents a challenge to the modern guarantee of inevitable progress. It takes Auschwitz and Hiroshima seriously as cautions against the uncritical belief in technological salvation. It encourages us instead to select and conjugate different aspects of the historical past, present and future. Thus ends the Hegelian version of History as a colossus marching relentlessly from a decadent Past towards a millenarian Tomorrow. History is now seen as a two-way street where we travel freely backward and forward.

In the specifically Irish context, this postmodern attitude to history might find expression, for example, in a retrieval and reinterpretation of certain positive features or high points of our premodern culture. One could cite here how early Ireland functioned without any centralised system of government or how the fascinating practice of *circumnavigatio*, based on voyage tales, informed the life of the medieval period. These traditions of political diversity and cultural circulation meant that Ireland was for many centuries a focal point of open-ended migration. It was a land which constantly received 'foreigners' into its midst and constantly sent forth its 'native' people to other lands. Premodern Ireland was an endless succession of invasions and expeditions, of import and export, immigration and emigration. In all aspects—political, religious and historical—Ireland proved to be a mixed culture of open circulation. We received a rich variety of cultures from abroad while many of our finest missionaries, thinkers and artists travelled to other lands to fulfil and communicate their talents. This 'circumnavigational' pattern of our tradition, this motif of perpetual exploration, of constant exodus and return, is held in a significant memory which ratifies and guides the postmodern model or *collage* as a blending of diverse perspectives. Departing from the ideology of national insularism, might we not once again reassert the positive advantages of our interdependence and interconnectedness with other cultures? And so doing, could we not endorse the vision of AE when he wrote: 'We do not want uniformity in our culture, but the balancing of our diversities in a wide tolerance. The moment we had complete uniformity our national life would be stagnant'?

VIII

What might be the *political* implications of this postmodern project? We would have to consider here two separate fronts: internal and external. A movement towards decentralised regional government *within* the nation would be correlative to a widening of our political life and awareness *beyond* the boundaries of the nation-state.

At the level of *internal* politics, a postmodern Ireland might be one which operated a policy of open consensus—a policy which encouraged a wide plurality of views and active participation from the different communities and traditions within our society. The consequences of this for the Northern conflict are obvious enough. It would mean a movement away from the stereotypes of ideological uniformity—Protestant Unionism in the North and Catholic Nationalism in the South—in the direction of a vigorous consensus politics where each voice, no matter how small or marginal, has a hearing. Consensus politics, thus understood, is the very basis of participatory democracy.

This does not mean an abandonment of our intellectual, political and religious heritage. But it does mean recognising that this heritage is not homogeneous, that it comprises a complex mix of different currents which may be rearranged in a new configuration—adding, where appropriate, radically new ideas from other entirely non-Irish cultures. Thus, for instance, we could draw discriminatingly from what is best in our inherited political traditions—the liberalism of Burke, Toland and Enlightenment Protestantism; the critical socialism of Thompson, Connolly and Larkin; the progressive republicianism of the United Irishmen; the emancipatory and scholarly heritage of the Catholic missionary tradition (which left monasteries and Irish colleges scattered throughout Europe and, in more recent times, has taken up the cause of the dispossessed in Central America and other oppressed regions of the world).

129

The postmodern model of consensual pluralism challenges the obsession with parliamentary uniformity. It opposes the traditional fetish of 'stable government'—the model of a copperfastened majority rule which disregards minorities by ensuring that there be no 'thinking otherwise'. The cult of political stability, thus understood, is the siamese twin of centralised power. And the ultimate in this kind of stability is dictatorship.

Two of the most 'stable' governments in Ireland's recent history have proved to be its worst. The first was called Stormont which effectively served as a Protestant Parliament for a Protestant People. And the second (though by no means as malign) was the Fianna Fáil government in the sixties which held unchallenged power for some sixteen years without any real opposition. Such hegemonic governments were symptomatic of what John Healy has called the 'stability of stagnation'. A shake-up of party politics in Ireland should not be in the direction of a *unification* of all parties within a centralised single party government(a Green Dáil answering to the old Orange Stormont). It should lead, rather, to a dissemination of power from the centre to the regions. Genuine democracy operates not on the basis of one group dominating over others, but on the basis of a consensus of many *different* voices.

The argument for a decentralised Ireland is not without precedent. There was the pioneering campaign for a co-operative movement conducted by Horace Plunkett and George Russell at the turn of the century; and, later, Alfred Ó Rahilly's crusade in the thirties for a decentralised Irish federation of counties. There have also been various proposals for a new constitution which would reverse the current trend toward centralised bureaucracy in the direction of greater regional participation in decision making—e.g. Sean MacBride's call for 32 local parliaments in 1980 and the proposals for regional and district government made by members of the Constitutional Reform Project in 1986-7. And finally there is the report on region-alisation, *Towards A New Democracy* by T.P. Barrington and Tom Walsh, commissioned by Muintir na Tíre. Whereas the arguments for the decentralisation of power from nation-state bureaucracies to regional communities have had little impact to date on our national parliament, they have received a very promising response in the European Community where MEPs such as John Hume, Eileen Lemass, Mary Banotti, Tom O'Donnell and Brendan Halligan have argued the case for increased regional develop-ment, at both urban and rural levels. The great break came in October, 1987 when Strasbourg passed the Hume Report on regionalisation by 250 votes to nil. As an *Irish Times* leading columnist commented: 'Political historians may well look back on the European Parliament's October session as the session when the political gap between Crete, Achill Island, Cape Clear—the so-called periphery of the EEC—became the equal of the wealthy centre; when the small lone voices of the edge of the Community won parity with the centre of power and the concept of a Europe, strong in all its parts, moved towards realisation'.[11]

The movement towards regionalisation at an *infra-national* level needs to be duly complemented by increased connections with other regional communities at a *trans-national* level. Hence the curious paradox that local customs, vernacular traditions and minority languages (such as Irish or Breton for example) are more likely to be culti-vated in a transnational federation of decentralised communities than in a centralised nation state.[12] Similarly, questions of minority rights and civil liberties are more likely to be respected in a transnational rather than a national tribunal—as Ireland's experience in the European Community and Council has already indicated. What is necessary is to secure a balance between the movement towards regionalisation *within* the nation and towards association *beyond* the nation.

The extremes of parochial chauvinism and anonymous uniformity are equally undesirable. Between the valley of the squinting windows and the no-man's-land of Las Vegas there is another way.

IX

A postmodern Ireland would encourage a radical pluralism not only inside its frontiers but also outside. If we examine our position in Europe, for example, a number of possibilities for political pluralism become apparent. There can be no doubt that more encouragement for regional development has come from Brussels and Strasbourg than from Dáil Éireann. Thus while several Irish thinkers have, as noted, argued the virtues of decentralised government in recent decades, it was not until John Hume recently presented his 'Report on the Regional Problems of Ireland' to the EEC that such proposals were seriously considered for the first time. And it is surely ironic that many of those who champion decentralisation (MacBride, Fennell, Crotty) have vigorously campaigned against our increased participation in that very European forum which has been the first to take decentralisation seriously. The Hume report urges that Ireland be divided into nine regions, each directly funded from the European Community rather than through a central state fund. However much of the proposal is realised, what is clear is that a transnational political forum in Europe is providing Ireland with the possibility of a major debate on the socio-economic future of our island. And what is additionally encouraging is that such a debate is being conducted in terms removed from civil-war ideologies and the shibboleths of the Ireland-England conflict. Rather than discussing our political future *for* ourselves alone or *against*

Britain, we now have the opportunity to do so in a context where we cease to be merely an adjunct or adversary of Britain and actively co-operate with eleven other communities—communities who have similar needs to transcend the limits of the nation-state model and to explore a postmodern model of interrelating decentralised regions.

The European Community, rather than being dismissed as a superstate bureaucracy in Brussels, added on to an already top-heavy bureaucracy in Dublin, might be positively regarded (in a postmodern context) as an opportunity to look beyond national borders and review the whole question of regional reorganisation. By looking *outside* the nation we might better be able to reconsider the problems *within* the nation. Indeed, it should not be forgotten that the European Parliament in Strasbourg is the only roof that has been able to house all the different political traditions of this island. It is in Strasbourg rather than in Leinster House, Stormont or Westminster, that John Hume and the MEPs from the Republic have been able to sit down with Ian Paisley and John Taylor and vote together in their common interests (something neither the Anglo-Irish Conference nor the Dublin Forum, despite their many virtues, has been able to achieve to date). And apart from their concerted approach on matters of regional funding, they have also made common cause in applying European safety measures to nuclear energy testing in Britain. Released from the antagonisms of nation-state politics, the trans-national forum of Europe has been able to provide some accord, however modest, on the infranational problems of Ireland.

The Hillsborough agreement was, of course, already an indication that the parties of Irish nationalism (at least) were prepared to enter into an international agreement with a neighbouring nation. And this readiness to transcend tribal conflicts by extending our horizon of consciousness and communications beyond the boundaries of the nation-state

133

has been further evidenced in the positive attitude of the Irish to the European Community. Irish nationalism has a relatively clean historical record—compared with most other European nationalisms (e.g. Germany and Spain)—as an ideology that has *defended* the rights of an oppressed community. If, however, it continues as the dominant ideology of the Republic it may degenerate (as did Unionism) into an assertion of triumphal superiority, predicated upon a manifest right of Destiny, to the exclusion of the rights of other traditions and communities. The disregard for minority rights shown in recent referenda surely signals such a danger. Beyond the extreme alternatives of traditional nationalism (which sees us as a nation apart) and modern 'multi-nationalism' (which sees us as a convenient haven for late capitalist expansion) there is another way: a postmodern transnationalism which would enable us to affirm our neutrality in an active manner while participating energetically in the larger community of Europe. Instead of seeing Europe as a supermarket for free give-aways, we would be better advised to explore what we have to con-tribute to Europe and, by extension, the world at large. We need more intervention and less of the *béal bocht*. If we are to have any sense of self-esteem in the larger world we must be as ready to give as to take.

X

The vexed question of our neutrality is central here. What is required, surely, is a sense of *positive neutrality*. As Michael D. Higgins said in the debate on the Single European Act referendum, there is no point in talking of our 'traditional neutrality' as one talks of traditional Irish corned beef and cabbage. Neutrality is not a sacred charm which safeguards us from external commitments. And it should not be invoked to disguise an *absence* of policy or to shore up some sort of we're-alright-Jack indifference. Positive neutrality means that we enter into world negotiations in the various international forums available to us—the UN and the European Community in particular—in order to provide an alternative view to the hegemony of the geo-political power blocs (and their military off-shoots e.g. NATO and the Warsaw Pact). In addition, it means forging new affiliations with other neutral and non-aligned countries throughout the world actively committed to peace and disarmament. To take the controversial question of our relation to the European Community on matters of foreign policy, surely we are more likely to influence international opinion by vigorous intervention in the community debates on disarmament, Central America, East-West relations etc. than by huddling on the sidelines in self-congratulatory monologue? We have proved our capacity for this kind of intervention in the UN. There is no reason why we should be any less confident of our ability for it in the European context. European political co-operation should not, and does not, mean a uniform EEC defence policy.

Playing a constructive role on the international stage is not, of course, going to be served by rhetorical posturing. We can only make a real impact at this level if we replace high-sounding debates with new ideas which are rigorously researched, inventive and realisable. Ideas and images have always been counted amongst Ireland's most valuable exports. We have contributed much to Europe and to the wider world in this regard. But to take a place in the vanguard of the postmodern movement, as I am suggesting, means being able to translate innovative cultural ideas into practicable policies of change.

A crucial means of promoting such policies is to fully exploit our interdependence in relation to other communities with similar objectives. It is not by locking ourselves into solitary confinement, with the Irish Sea as some kind of *cordon sanitaire*, that we will alter anything. Our best chance of affecting international policy in the interests of peace is to voice an assertive position on world affairs. In an IMS poll taken in May 1984, 84 per cent of respondents stated that Ireland should remain neutral in order to do all in its power to ease the tensions between the USA and the USSR. The most effective way of realising this wish is for Ireland to interconnect with other like-minded communities throughout the globe, using the extraordinary potential of the trans-national communications network to pursue a disarmament crusade. Ireland Alone is a nation deaf and dumb—a nation so preoccupied with its own internal purity that it is unprepared to risk contagion by intervening in the international scene to effect real change. Such an Ireland is neither desirable nor feasible.

XI

One of the shortcomings to date of Irish discussion of the European Community has been the almost exclusive emphasis on the economic dimension. It is undeniable that Ireland has obtained notable economic benefits from the EEC—John Hume's successful campaign for a £70 million investment in regional development in the North and the granting of £80 million to the Republic in 1986 being conspicuous cases in point. It is also tragically true, as the leader of the Labour Party, Dick Spring, argued during the SEA debate, that with one in five out of work and 50,000 leaving Ireland each year, our nation does not at present have the wealth, markets or opportunities to survive *on its own*. But that does not mean that we should try to solve Ireland's unemployment problem by exporting it to Europe, waving an ECU wand to convert the Irish lumpen proletariat into a gaggle of high-tech Wild Geese. The perception of Europe as a multi-national economy where capital may indiscriminately flow has simply fuelled the arguments of those who denounce the European Community as a 'rich man's club'—a haven for endless commodification based on consumerist 'Euro-values' at odds with the ideals of the nation's Founding Fathers. This perception has frequently blinded people to the positive implications of a Europe open to the free circulation of its citizens and workforce. It also ignores that the largest grouping in the EEC is the socialist one; and that there exists a significant movement at present in Brussels and Strasbourg away from centralised bureaucracy and towards a radical form of regional democracy.

If there is a genuine future for Irish socialism, it lies, I believe, within the context of a new, decentralised Europe, as Michael D. Higgins, chairman of the Labour Party, argued in his address on Regional Policy to the Socialist Group of the European Parliament (10 September 1987): 'We must affirm the principle that Article 23 of the Single European Act is primarily aimed at creating a Single Europe of equals...equality and egalitarianism were never under greater threat. A true regional policy could be one instrument for releasing the great human potential that socialist society promises.' And he adds that 'those socialists who reject the challenge will have brought themselves, inheritors of older, braver struggles, close to the dustbin of history'.[13]

In these respective pleas for practical and concrete measures to create a new Europe of social justice, decentralised into regions on an egalitarian basis, John Hume and Michael D. Higgins (amongst others) have been giving contemporary credence to Voltaire's noble dream of Europe as 'a kind of great republic divided into equal parts...each one corresponding with the other'.[14]

The practices of massive fish dumping and food accumulation in order to meet EEC quotas and balance sheets are, of course, scandalous. But the best way to remedy such

137

indefensible market policies is not to decry them from afar but to get in there and change things. That is what democracy means. And the European Community is a democracy. If and when the desired change towards decentralisation comes, it will be as a result of a two-pronged campaign—one from the alternative movements on the 'margins' of the political system; and the other from certain parliamentary groupings at the very centre of power who have come to the recognition that the future of a genuine European community lies in the withering away of state and super-state bureaucracy in favour of regional democracy. Between the extremes of state bureaucracy and individualist enterprise exists the possibility of a *public* sphere which is genuinely communitarian and pluralist.[15]

Moreover, belonging to Europe is not just an economic matter. It also involves political and cultural citizenship. Some of the political possibilities have been alluded to above in our discussion on neutrality. In conclusion, I would like to say something about the advantages of becoming *cultural* citizens of Europe and the international scene generally. (And as Jean Monet observed, 'L'Europe sera culturelle ou ne sera pas.') One of the main virtues of such citizenship is that it permits decentralisation without provincialisation. To actively engage in the process of European interdependence should not be seen as a movement towards uniformity where Ireland, and other smaller nations, would be reduced to the status of a province totally dependent on a new geo-political power centre located in Brussels. This would mean that we had shaken off our former provincial relations with the British Empire only to ensnare ourselves in new provincial relations with Euro-Empire (on a par with the imperial power-centres of the US and the USSR). If such were the case, Ireland's political citizenship in Europe would be a form of self-induced serfdom, while our cultural citizenship would be as vacuous as the Eurovision song contest.

But this need not be the case. Membership of Europe means belonging to a multi-racial, multi-lingual network of communities comprising some 220 million people and several dozen nationalities (minorities included). Viewed in the context of postmodern pluralism, this signals a movement towards diversity rather than uniformity, a renewed appreciation of cultural difference rather than a slide into some kind of totalitarian sameness. A postmodern Europe fully exploiting the decentralising potential of the new communications network should be construed not as a geo-political empire made up of servilely dependent provinces but as a multi-form community of communities. Such a postmodern Europe is, of course, not a *fait accompli*. It is a task still to be accomplished.

XII

In a postmodern Europe the national preoccupation with emigration and immigration could be superseded by the positive model of *migration*. The enormous opportunities for greater circulation across national boundaries should be exploited by small nations like Ireland whose literate and skilled young generations have much to contribute to Europe, much to learn there, and much to bring back again. (And higher education qualifications should be available to everybody in Ireland regardless of class or income.) This is not idle utopianism. After all, is it not in the interests of every taxpaying citizen to provide as many young people as possible with an advanced education (rather than the mere consolation of the dole queue)? And surely if those who *choose* to go abroad for work do so with a qualification, their chances of succeeding there and of making a positive Irish contribution to other societies will be significantly enhanced.

Furthermore, those Irish emigrés who feel grateful and

proud of the 'home education' which prepared them for success abroad are far more likely to *return* to Ireland with new ideas, as soon as circumstances permit. Freedom and mobility of mind, as fostered by a good education at home and openness to other cultures and societies, is clearly one of the best means of creating solutions to the many problems—economic and otherwise—which have brought about the present crisis in Irish society. The days of uniquely Irish solutions to uniquely Irish problems are over. If we are to make the migratory model effective, if we are to create a climate to which the Irish abroad would wish to return, it is necessary to recognise that people leave Ireland for two main reasons: *economic*—they cannot earn an adequate living; and *cultural*—Irish society today is simply not dynamic and innovative enough.*

XIII

This picture of a postmodern Europe—and even of a post-modern world—as an open-frontier community of communities, requires that our view of ourselves and of others change. It encourages us to cease vacillating between isolationism and grievance and assume our full responsibilities as an equal member of the international community. In this respect, perhaps the 'identity crisis' which has dominated Irish cultural circles in recent years should be seen in a new light: not as a self-obsessive quest for a lost national essence, but as a basic dissatisfaction with the inherited ideologies of identity which sufficed up to now. So viewed, the crisis could actually open up alternative horizons of understanding ourselves and others. Thus instead of remaining trapped in the endgames of self-identity and self-consciousness, we might be able to affirm our identity not as some sacrosanct substance but as a *collage* of diverse relations. The question of identity would cease to be a matter of narcissistic navel-gazing and reveal itself as an open-ended project inextricably bound up with the identities of others. A genuine sense of belonging is often most acutely experienced in the encounter with other peoples and places.

Our voice needs to be heard in the global village of post-modern culture. We have much to contribute. And we have much to receive. Talking to oneself is tedious; and it convinces no one. To go it alone is to go nowhere. The post-modern condition is already ours. Whether we like it or not, the twin modern ideologies of the centralised nation-state and the autonomous consumer individual no longer convince. These models which have guided modern western society in recent centuries, appear to be in a state of imminent redundancy. The challenge is to devise a post-modern project to respond to this time of transition in a positive way.

*The postmodern model of radical pluralism outlined above should address at least the second of these factors, by making for a society to which people would wish to return. And such a reflux of Irish minds as well as an influx of non-Irish minds (which an open postmodern society would foster) might further advance a genuine resolution of our economic and ideological problems. Thus the one-way ticket of emigration could be replaced by the two-way ticket of migration, movement abroad being seen as provisional detour rather than permanent exile (in contrast to the period from the nineteenth-century famines to the nineteen fifties). It might be seen too as a positive opportunity for mutual enrichment by Irish and non-Irish communities rather than a token of failure and rejection. Professor John McCarthy has observed: 'The fact that significant numbers of Irishmen and women will make their livings in Amsterdam, Bonn and Venice ought seem no more a tragedy than the number of Nebraskans or Arkansans who wind up in Southern California, Chicago or New Orleans. Indeed given the demographic statistics of much of Western Europe...the ultimate will be some time in the future when second or third generation Irish will become Burgomeisters of Essen or Frankfurt.' To promote migration is *not* to condone emigration. Those who argue that to accept emigration is to acquiesce in 'national suicide' are correct. The postmodern model of migration is to be seen rather as a radical *alternative* to the scandal of emigration in Ireland today where 30,000 citizens are compelled into exile each year. One of its primary aims is to create a society where movement abroad is a choice, not a necessity, and where those who have been forced into exile may be 'called home', to use Peader O'Donnell's phrase in his famous attack on emigration in the forties (*The Bell*, Feb. 1945). But they should be called home because there is a home worth returning to, and worth welcoming citizens of other lands to join.

141

6. *Ireland and the European Community-Progress in Common or Decline Together*

I N January 1988 Ireland celebrated the fifteenth anniversary of membership of the European Community. Fifteen years is a very short span to encompass the kind of change which the country has experienced. How do we assess the transformation which is taking place while we are still in the thick of it?

During the 1972 referendum an overwhelming majority of the Irish electorate voted to join the Community and this support has been maintained during the intervening years, as shown by the various surveys carried out by the European Commission and confirmed in the Referendum in May 1987 on the ratification of the Single European Act. The European Community is growing. Ireland's relationship with the Community is maturing and the attitudes of the Irish to their own country and to the larger community of which they are part are changing. This fifteenth anniversary is therefore a most suitable occasion for reflection on how Ireland as a nation has performed and where we see ourselves going over the next fifteen years which will take us into the twenty-first century.

The facts are easily stated. In 1973, Ireland along with the United Kingdom and Denmark, joined a Community of six nations which formed a cohesive bloc in western Europe and, with the addition of Greece in 1981 and Spain and Portugal in 1986, a Community of 320 million people was established. Within that, Ireland represents just over 1 per cent of the population and contributes a very small proportion of the total domestic product of the Community. In contrast, Ireland represents one-twelfth of the Council of Ministers, has approximately 4 per cent of the weighted voting system and Irish representatives (from the Republic only) represent approximately 3 per cent of the membership of the European Parliament.

Industrial production in Ireland between 1973 and 1986 has risen steeply and this has been accompanied by a rise in exports to the rest of the Community. There has been a change in the pattern of our trade because, while trade with our traditional market—the United Kingdom—rose tenfold, that with other members of the Community rose thirtyfold. For the United Kingdom, which was our predominant partner in our trade relations before 1973—with over 70 per cent of imports and exports coming from and going to the United Kingdom—the corresponding percentages are now approximately halved and while Britain remains Ireland's main market, and is likely to continue to do so, many new markets have been opened in other member states of the Community and they represent together 38 per cent of total Irish exports.

Although unemployment has risen dramatically since 1973 (world recession and our own population boom being contributory factors) nonetheless total employment has risen by over 20,000 jobs in the period since accession.

The direct economic benefit from the Community has also been dramatic: the net contributions from the Community of over £6.5 billion have made a substantial contribution to the development of our physical infrastructure, the re-adaptation of our labour force to take on new skills and the substantial restructuring of agriculture. The multiplier effect of this transfer from the Community cannot be minimised.

143

There has been in Ireland, however, a concentration on these figures almost to the total exclusion of all other considerations of our membership of the European Community. The corollary of concentration on these 'beneficial' figures has been an opposition which blames all the economic and social ills of the country on membership of the Community. But this assessment is also too simplistic, and underneath the rather glib statements about economic benefit there is a desire among Irish people to be part of the movement towards European integration and a realisation that we could and should make a greater contribution than we have done up to now. There are many whose reservations are not about membership itself but about the future of the Community, its place in the world and our role in its evolution.

Ireland, being an island on the periphery of the Community, was not affected directly by the trauma and upheaval of the Second World War in the same way as the states of central and north western Europe. We must never forget (and there are those today who do tend to forget) that the origins of our present-day Community lie in those horrific years between 1939 and 1948 when Europe, having gone through another world war, lay prostrate and the people of Europe experienced hunger and hopelessness.

Ireland did not participate in the process of integration throughout the late 1940s and the 1950s and our insulation from what was happening could be seen in the newspaper coverage of the signing of the Treaty of Rome on the 25th March 1957. Comment was confined to a small news item in one Irish national newspaper. At that time our links were, and had been for many years, largely with Britain and the United States, where hundreds of thousands—indeed millions—of our people had settled over the years. That settlement by Irish people created a network of contacts between families and individuals which was to remain, and will remain for some time to come, a very potent force for our people. The ease of contact because of language ensured that trade also followed that flow of emigration. The fact also that we are close to a very large and powerful neighbour, that we speak the same language as that neighbour and share to a very large extent in its cultural development through newspapers, radio and, more latterly and in a more powerful way, television, serves to keep our vision, to a very large extent, in that direction.

This is not to say that there was no contact with what we call 'Europe'. Over the centuries there have been relationships with mainland Europe and there is no need to document them. However, over the last 200 years the contacts were very tenuous and only affected a very small number of people—for the most part clergy, writers and some politicians.

Accession to the European Community, therefore, came upon Ireland as something of a shock, leading to a sudden expansion of our horizons as a country. Suddenly, we were faced with a new set of partners, a system of networks to be constructed, and we were joining a Community where the predominant language was not English but French. We had to provide civil servants to staff the Institutions of the Community, and a number of organisations from Ireland suddenly had to think of their interests in a new atmosphere and to consider opening up offices on the European mainland, something which had seldom arisen in the past. The numbers involved may not have been very great but the impact was quite substantial.

What was the Community which Ireland joined and what was its attitude to Ireland? For the most part the original member states of the Community viewed Ireland in a positive way. Here was a small country with a very chequered history, a history that was for the most part well known in general terms in western Europe, a relatively poor country by

145

the then standards of the existing European Community and yet not big enough to make any major impact on the overall resources of the Community. Its people were seen to be humorous, attractive and with a 'joie de vivre' quite different from that of the industrialised parts of western Europe. The fact that Ireland was predominantly English-speaking and was a parliamentary democracy—a democracy which had been established by emerging from an almost colonial-type system through a war of independence and a civil war—was also an attractive factor to the countries of the Community; the fact that Ireland was joining at the same time as the United Kingdom was also seen as an advantage since a major attraction of Britain joining the Community, apart from economic and political aspects, was its parliamentary tradition, seen as a major stabilising factor in the development of the Community. Ireland was expected to strengthen the contribution of the United Kingdom while being sufficiently different to provide a bridge between Britain and the mainland—the legacy of the Common Law and the Napoleonic Code.

It should be said that one of the great disappointments in the early years of the United Kingdom's membership of the Community was the lack of total commitment to that membership and the wrangling which emerged in the first ten years of membership. The Socialist and Social Democratic Parties were particularly disillusioned by the attitude of the British Labour Party at that time.

The goodwill towards Ireland was underpinned during the negotiations by the attitudes which Ireland took to the adaptation to Community law, and of course the very strong pro-vote in the referendum of 1972 was a major factor in giving the Irish a reputation for being 'communitaire'.

While the provisions of the Treaty and the representation of Ireland in the various institutions are one side of the story, it is by no means the whole story— the high participation of

Ireland in various grants given by the Community is not a result only of regulation and law. Those grants are there because there is an understanding of Ireland's position and there is a sympathy which has been very important as the Community has developed. The contribution made by the early 'pioneers' going into the Community cannot be over-stated and Irishmen and women have made a substantial impact on all the Community institutions. The younger generation coming in now will have to extend that impact. Only a small number worked directly with the Community institutions. They led the way, however, and slowly Irishmen and women are beginning to see the Community countries of mainland Europe are being part of their future. But why has it been so slow?

The lack of contact with the developing European Community during the 1950s and 1960s and the concentration on the financial benefits of joining the Community tended to give the Irish public a limited view of what the Community is about. The articles which appear in the Irish media tend to concentrate on those things which affect only Ireland and this reflects to some extent the attitudes at all levels in administration and in Irish society. During the referendum on the Single European Act, the debate on European Political Co-operation exposed the narrowness of view among Irish people—quite surprising in a country with such a far-flung network of exiles throughout the world. The message seemed to be coming across that we could somehow build a wall around the country and ignore what is happening in the world at large. This appears too, even at official level some-times, when the Irish Ministers are not expected to comment on certain items on the Community agenda because they have no immediate impact on Ireland. One comment has been made, however, by a former Minister, dealing with affairs in the European Community, when he asked, 'How can we expect other countries to take an interest in us if we do not take an interest in them?'

Our view of the Community often tends to be a narrow and, indeed, selfish view. Being members of a community does not mean that you only pick out the things that are of interest or are beneficial to yourself. It means there is an obligation to look at the totality of relationships and to be part of the development of all those relationships. We seldom see or hear anything in the Irish media about how other people live in the Community nor how we can learn from them. For the most part our partners are highly industrialised countries with a density of population much greater than our own. They have many problems, some of which we share, but they have also survived crises through which we, as an increasingly urbanised country, will also pass, and we could possibly learn from them how best to do so. Indeed, there are many aspects of straightforward social organisation that we could learn from a number of our European partners, particularly the smaller countries. While we in Ireland do not, in my view, work less hard than people in other member states, overall the management and organisation of our society leaves a lot to be desired and we could improve the social and economic effectiveness of the money we spend and get better results from the energy we expend if we took some lessons from our partners.

Ireland has gone through a social revolution in the last twenty-five years, and particularly the last fifteen years—we have moved from being a highly rural society to an industrialised urban society. Any who can cast their minds back twenty-five years to remember the sort of society we then had, the standard of housing, the general standard of living, can only be impressed by the fact that in that time we have moved from what could be described as a village economy to an urban economy. Part of our problem, however, is that the rules of social organisation have not changed and we are running an urban economy on the rules of the village. This is not in any way a criticism of the village economy, but as we

develop we have to change to meet new needs and new challenges. We have not yet come to terms with the problems of
urban life and we tend to feel that a city is really the country
with all the houses pushed together. In reality they are two
quite different entities.

There is also a feeling in Ireland that the status quo of yes-
terday must be the status quo of today, the status quo of
tomorrow and indeed the status quo of the week after next.
While change is taking place in the way we live, we do not
appear to be prepared to adapt our social organisation to deal
with it or, if we do, we accept it only slowly.

During the general election in Ireland of February 1987
there was considerable criticism of the coverage by the
foreign press on the campaign. There were comments that
Ireland was a Third World country. These were resented, not
only by politicians of all shades of opinion but by many
ordinary Irish people. Unfortunately, many of the comments
about being a Third World country came from Irish people
themselves and were picked up by foreign journalists. But if
at the end of February 1987 you considered the plight of a
German, French or Dutch correspondent coming to Ireland
for the first time and driving from the airport into Dublin
and then on to Cork, you would have to describe the impact
of his first impressions: he would have seen a complete disregard for the traffic laws—people parked in positions where
they inconvenience twenty, thirty or forty others, people
driving through red lights (a common sight), people not
wearing seat belts and driving at night on country roads
where they meet heavy goods vehicles with defective
lighting, and total chaos during the day in our country towns
due to bad traffic control.

These may seem trivial issues but they reflect a lack of
concern for others and a disrespect for laws which are set
down for social organisation. If there is such a disrespect for
laws and the rights of others in this rather obvious area, a

foreign correspondent must ask himself what is the situation *vis-à-vis* other aspects of society in other areas and the social responsibilities that people feel in these other areas. But these are problems of change and the management of change. Irish people are no more and no less law-abiding than people in other countries, but there are sanctions, both legal and social, which are not applied in Ireland. In a rural society it did not matter all that much where a car or a van was parked—speed was slower, space was plentiful: it did not matter if a radio was played at full blast—the nearest neighbour was well out of earshot. But in an urban environment, these things become important and other people are affected.

The management of society itself has not changed with changing times—it is very difficult to explain to non-Irish people how you could design an administrative system which allows 30 per cent of cars to drive without insurance when the percentage in a country such as Belgium is probably less than 1 per cent. It is also difficult to explain how so many of our public institutions work hours which have not changed since the early part of this century, even though, again, our society has changed dramatically. There is another side to the coin, however; when things have to be done well they are done well and there are many instances in Ireland where there is a caring management, and our standards are as high as any in the world. But the pursuit of excellence is not fundamental in our society. Sustained effort has to be supported and excellence cannot be maintained without an adequate supporting culture and structure. Many of our partners have evolved such structures in certain areas and this is something we can learn from them.

We can learn. We should learn. But some of what we learn from the partners is what we should not do. Some countries have an inflexibility to society which is just as disheartening and frustrating as the shortcomings I have cited in Ireland.

Often they bring forward planning to such a high degree that there can be no flexibility while we in Ireland have that flexibility allied to a sense of humour and we should try to maintain and find a balance between efficiency and the extreme where the plan or the programme itself is an end in itself.

In learning more about the organisation and way of life of our partners we can, I feel, learn more about the opportunities that there are for Ireland and for Irish people. It must be said that the very dramatic growth in trade between Ireland and the rest of the Community, excluding the United Kingdom, conceals the fact that native Irish companies have not exploited market opportunities to anything like their full potential.

In global terms, 34 per cent of Irish exports in 1986 went to the UK, 38 per cent went to the Continental EEC countries. However, a recent Irish Export Board survey of 1,000 companies showed that 43 per cent of total exports of Irish-owned firms went to the UK market, while 25 per cent went to the other EEC countries.

So there is considerable scope for development—not in abandoning traditional markets but rather in concentrating on the expansion possibilities that exist in the wider European market which it is hoped will become a truly integrated market by 1992. Ireland's share of German imports amounted to 0.76 per cent in 1986 (which represented an increase since 1981) while the corresponding figures for France were 0.55 per cent, Netherlands 0.59 per cent and Italy 0.24 per cent. There appears to be considerable scope for expansion but there are obstacles—the size of native Irish companies is one and language is probably another.

We tend to delude ourselves that we are not good at languages and consequently we cannot learn them. Nothing could be further from the truth. If a person wants to do something and do it well, they can usually do it, and this is true of learning another language. But to truly learn another language means that a person has to live in the country where that language is spoken and in learning the language become familiar not just with the rules, not just with grammatical expression, but also with the culture behind that language. The knowledge gained is an essential part of the whole process of selling in a marketplace and we have not yet begun to do that. Learning a language is, admittedly, expensive, but our commitment to languages must begin in school.

A very strong campaign should be launched and resources allocated to ensure that every student finishes second-level education with a good working knowledge of at least one, if not two, European languages because within a Community now of nine languages, we should consider knowledge of at least two, plus mother tongue, as being an essential part of the education of every young Irish boy and young Irish girl. Translating that knowledge into hard practical use is the next stage and the way has been shown by the conversion of the Irish College at Louvain, long an educational establishment of the Irish Province of the Franciscan Order, into the Irish Institute for European Affairs. Here, young Irish men and women are introduced to many aspects of life in continental Europe as well as the workings of the European Community. The course which equips young people for marketing in Europe, for example, has been an outstanding success. The numbers involved are admittedly small but it is an indication of the way things can go. There must be a commitment at all levels—Government, industry, trade unions and the educational establishment, to ensure that every opportunity available for young people in the Community is fully exploited.

We have the anomalous situation of thousands of our young people in the United States who have entered illegally and who are continually looking over their shoulder to ensure they keep one step ahead of the immigration authorities whereas, on the other hand, here is a community of 320 million people where they can move freely and with all the rights of the natives of those countries. In Germany the number of deaths annually now outstrips births and there is a major problem looming for the Germans—to find enough people to man industry and services. Ireland has a young population, well-educated, who could take those jobs, but the vital link must be made and that link is language.

Our contribution to the development of the Community can be substantial, much greater than our numbers would suggest. Already, in the field of music, Ireland is well known, particularly in north-western Europe. The Chieftains have no trouble whatsoever in filling a hall with enthusiastic French, Belgians, Germans or Dutch, wherever they may appear, while at the other end of the music scale, U2 and Chris de Burgh are equally recognised. In theatre we have a long history but yet, to a large extent, we have tended to ignore mainland Europe.

Television has also charted a path in a small way. Some of RTE's best programmes have been taken up by European networks, and we now see the beginnings of an emerging film industry in Ireland with young actors, producers and directors beginning to make their mark on the international scene. We should not forget radio, a relatively inexpensive means of communication, which can also allow us to link up more and more with our European partners to learn more about them and to let them learn more about us.

But this development will not take place on its own, it has to be encouraged and there has to be a conscious decision made to move into mainstream Europe and perhaps it is from the State-sponsored bodies, like RTE and the Arts Council that the main thrust should begin to come. It would pay substantial dividends.

Most of all, we need in this country to think of ourselves as

Europeans at all levels of society. However, this is not going to happen overnight and, if it is allowed to develop on its own, will not happen as fast as it should. It will not be easy to turn the eyes of our young people towards Europe, to see their future there, unless those who are older, and those who make decisions, are prepared to change too.

As I have already said, language is one key factor in the pull of our young people to the US, Australia, Canada and the UK, but the networks of relatives and friends which exist in these countries are also very important. Similar networks only exist in Europe in a very very small way, and so it is the true trail-blazers who make their way into Europe. However, there are now communities of Irish people in Paris, Brussels, Amsterdam, Dusseldorf, Frankfurt, and elsewhere, and the informal contacts which are built up through these communities are extremely important for people coming for the first time into these cities.

We should now think of going a stage further and supporting these communities as part of the European network through which our young people could pass as they gain experience and knowledge which they can use subsequently back in Ireland, or elsewhere, for the benefit of themselves and their country.

The experience at the Institute for European Affairs at Louvain perhaps points the way to other developments. There is an Irish College in Paris, premises outside Madrid have been offered to the Irish Government, there are possibilities in other European cities. Perhaps we should begin to develop these as a basis for introducing our people into mainland Europe with particular courses provided in each of them. Again, this will need initiatives at political level and will also need the expenditure of some monies—not very much, in my view, in relative terms—and the payback would be very substantial over coming decades.

A fundamental policy of the Community is to create a true

European Home Market by 1992. The first phase of building the community—abolishing tariffs between the member states and creating a common external tariff—was completed well within the time-scale provided in the original Treaty of Rome. But member states still maintained an array of non-tariff barriers to trade, ostensibly to protect health and safety but usually to protect the home market. In addition, while the goods could often move freely, the transport carrying them was subject to very strict protective rules, while differences in taxes and duties between member states added further costs to international trading. This has meant that the Community is made up of twelve fragmented markets and European industry has had to contend with meeting so many different rules and standards in the Community that its competitive position *vis-à-vis* its main trade competitors, the US and Japan, has diminished considerably, and has contributed to the sluggish economic growth over the past ten years.

The abolition of these non-tariff barriers to trade is seen as a *sine qua non* of reducing the Community economically. It is for this reason that the European Commission launched its programme in 1985 to eliminate the more than 300 non-tariff barriers by 1992. This programme has been accompanied by a major programme to harmonise standards in telecommunications and new information technology, a major programme for research and development in new technologies, and the launching of policy to eliminate barriers caused by controls in the transport industry.

Ireland stands to gain much from these changes if it is ready to seize the opportunities, and that means providing the goods and services needed by the market, of the best possible quality, and delivering them on time and hopefully in the languages appropriate to the various markets.

The next fifteen years will be crucial for the European Community. If the plans being initiated now are a success (and the achievement of that success will not be easy) then Europe will be able to move into a new era, capable of withstanding the growing competition not only in the world market but in the European market itself. Ireland can contribute to that success, and is already doing so in support of the Community's policies. We can look to the success of other small countries, both inside and outside the Community, in exploiting opportunities.

There are boundless opportunities in the economic field for Ireland and the Irish people but they will have to be achieved—they will not be handed on a plate. Exploiting these opportunities could bring back again the growth of the seventies and give the psychological boost that is so badly needed: it could get us to the stage where involuntary emigration could be once again eliminated and we could see again the phenomenon of former Irish emigrants—highly skilled and trained—coming back to contribute to Ireland's success in Europe.

There must be a conscious effort at national level to ensure that not only do we exploit all the opportunities and potential which exist in a growing European community, but that we play our full part in its development for ourselves and those who come after us.*

*The author is an employee of the Commission of the European Communities. The views expressed in this essay are the author's personal views and are not necessarily those of the European Commission.

Notes

Notes to 1. Patrick Honohan, **The Role of the Adviser and the Evolution of the Public Service**
1. Cf. my paper entitled 'Macroeconomic and Fiscal Deviations from Plan 1984-87', in *Perspectives on Economic Policy*, ed. D. R. Thom and C. Ó Gráda, 1987, UCD Centre for Economic Policy Research 1987.
2. Kevin Murphy, 'A Changing Civil Service?', *Administration*, 1986.
3. Ian Irvine and I have recently contributed to this debate in a paper entitled 'The Marginal Social Cost of Taxation in Ireland', submitted to the *Economic and Social Review*.
4. I refer in particular to the Statistical and Social Inquiry Society of Ireland's symposium in November 1983, and reported in the Society's Journal for 1983-84.
5. It might even have been possible for the Commission on Social Welfare to integrate its recommendations with those of the Commission on Taxation. I have discussed this possibility in a paper entitled, 'A Radical Reform of Social Welfare and Income Taxation Evaluated', in *Administration*, 1987.
6. This is despite the fact that, in the NESC Report of 1986, the 'social partners' endorse the thrust of the Commission on Taxation's Reports and call on Government to respond to the recommendations.
7. Cf. John Roden, Donal de Buitléir, Donal Ó Brolchain, 'A Design for Democracy', *Administration*, 1986.

Notes to 3. John Maguire, **The Case for a New Social Order**
1. F. Litton (ed.), *Unequal Achievement*, Dublin 1982.
2. C.T. Whelan and B.J. Whelan, *Social Mobility in the Republic of Ireland: A Comparative Perspective*, Dublin 1984.
3. D. Rottman and P. O'Connell, 'The Changing Social Structure' in Litton, op. cit, pp. 663-88; quotation is from p. 74.
4. M. Peillon, 'Stratification and Class' in P. Clancy *et al.* (eds.),

Ireland: A Sociological Profile, Dublin 1986, pp. 97-115; quotation is from p. 100.

5. Loc. cit., p. 83.
6. D. Rottman and D. Hannan, 'The Impact of State Taxation and Transfer Policies on Income Inequality in the Republic of Ireland', in M. Kelly *et al.* (eds.), *Power, Conflict and Inequality*, Dublin 1982, pp. 116-30, especially 129-30.
7. Loc. cit., p. 110.
8. F. Sammon, 'The Generation of Poverty in Ireland' in Council for Social Welfare, *Conference on Poverty 1981*, Dublin 1982, pp. 55-78; quotation is from p. 71.
9. Loc. cit., p. 74.
10. Loc. cit., p. 112.
11. See, e.g., loc. cit., p. 185.
12. M. Laver *et al.* (eds.), *How Ireland Voted*, Dublin 1987, p. 112.
13. A. Giddens, *The Class Structure of the Advanced Societies*, London 1973.
14. Loc. cit., p. 64.
15. See J. Blackwell, 'Government and Society' in Litton (ed.), op. cit., pp. 43-60; quotation is from p. 49; and, for 1987 figure cf. *Irish Times* 5 December 1987, p. 1.
16. M. Peillon, *Contemporary Irish Society: An Introduction*, Dublin 1982, p. 1.
17. Ibid., p. 182.
18. H. Tovey, 'Milking the Farmer? Modernisation and Marginalisation in Irish Dairy Farming', in Kelly *et al.* (eds.), op. cit., pp. 68-89; quotation is from p. 89.
19. See W.B. Gallie, 'Essentially Contested Concepts' in *Proceedings of the Aristotelian Society*, 56 (1955-56), pp. 167-98.
20. See K. Kumar, *Prophecy and Progress*, Penguin 1978, for a discussion of this distinction between images of society.
21. P. Commins, 'Rural Social Change' in Clancy *et al.* (eds.), op. cit., pp. 47-67; quotation is from p. 66.
22. J. Wickham, 'Industrialisation, Work and Unemployment' in Clancy *et al.*, (eds), op. cit., pp. 70-96.
23. J. Holland, 'The Poor's Challenge to the Church in a New Stage of World History' in Council for Social Welfare, op. cit., pp. 112-35; quotation is from p. 118.
24. I have examined some aspects of this referendum campaign in an unpublished lecture, 'The Irish Referendum on the Single

European Act, 1987' delivered to a seminar at the Vanderbilt Institute for Public Policy Studies, Vanderbilt University, USA, in September 1987.

25. K. Marx, in D. McLellan, *Karl Marx: His Life and Thought* 2nd edn London 1980, p. 184.
26. See C. Mouffe, 'Hegemony and Ideology in Gramsci' in idem (ed.) *Gramsci and Marxist Theory*, London 1979, pp. 168-204.
27. For an account of all these views, see S. Lukes, *Power: A Radical View*, London 1974.
28. Bachrach and Baratz, quoted in S. Lukes, op. cit., pp. 18-19.
29. D. Rottman *et al.*, *The Distribution of Income in the Republic of Ireland*, Dublin 1982, p. 182.
30. T. McCashin, 'Social Policy 1957-82' in Litton (ed.), op. cit., pp. 203-23; quotation is from p. 221.
31. T.K. Whitaker, 'Future Possibilities' in Council for Social Welfare, op. cit., pp. 102-11; quotation is from p. 109.
32. J. Lee, 'Society and Culture' in Litton (ed.), op. cit., pp. 1-18; quotation is from p. 2.
33. B. Ryan, 'Unemployment' in *Cork and the Wider World* No. 13, p. 3.
34. F. Sammon, loc. cit., pp. 67-8.
35. J.P. O'Carroll, 'Strokes, Cute Hoors and Sneaking Regarders: The Influence of Local Culture on Irish Political Style' in *Irish Political Studies* 2 (1987), pp. 77-92; quotation is from p. 83.
36. C. Curtin, and A. Varley, 'Children and Childhood in Rural Ireland: A Consideration of the Ethnographic Literature', in C. Curtin *et al.* (eds.), *Culture and Ideology in Ireland*, Galway 1984, pp. 30-45; quotation is from p. 43.
37. For a profound analysis of the impact of early childhood experience of cruelty and repression in later adult, including political, life, see the work of Alice Miller, particularly *For Your Own Good: Hidden Cruelty in Child-Rearing and the Roots of Violence*, London 1983.
38. See, for example, Socialist Economists Group, *Jobs and Wages—The True Story of Competitiveness*, Dublin 1983 and *Jobs and Borrowing: Where the Right is Wrong*, Dublin 1985; J. Brady, 'Wealth, Work and Employment' in *Studies* (Summer 1985), pp. 155-69, and A. Matthews, 'Economics and Ideology' in *The Crane Bag*, Vol. 9 No. 2 (1985), pp. 52-60. For a somewhat different critique and alternative, see also R. Crotty,

Ireland in Crisis, Dingle 1986.

39. Loc. cit.
40. J. Lee, loc. cit., pp. 7-8.
41. See S. Kalberg, 'Max Weber's Types of Rationality', *American Journal of Sociology* Vol. 85, No. 5 (1980), pp. 1145-79.
42. K. Theweleit, *Male Fantasies* (tr. S. Conway *et al.*), Polity Press, London 1987, p. 270.
43. On this and many other points of interest, see L. O'Dowd, 'Neglecting the Material Dimension: Irish Intellectuals and the Problem of Identity' in *The Irish Review*, 3, Cork U.P. (1988), pp. 8-17.
44. Karl Marx in D. McLellan, op. cit., p. 125.
45. Address entitled 'Development and Disarmament—A Southern Perspective' delivered to non-governmental organisation delegates at International Conference on the Relationship Between Disarmament and Development, United Nations, New York, 23 August—11 September 1987.
46. See Karl Marx, in D. McLellan, op. cit., p. 35.
47. B. Ehrenreich, Foreword to K. Theweleit, op. cit., pp. ix-xvii; quotation is from p. xvii.

Notes to 4. Peter Froggatt, **Business and Academia—the Fruitful Interaction of Town and Gown**
1. J.H. Newman, *The Idea of a University, Defined and Illustrated*, ed. C.F. Harrold, London: Longman, 1947.
2. T. Hobbes, *Leviathan: or the Matter, Forme and Power of a Commonwealth, Ecclesiasticall and Civill*, London: Crooke, 1651.
3. Sir Alex Jarratt, (Chairman), *Report of the Steering Committee for Efficiency Studies in Universities*, London: Committee of Vice-chancellors and Principals, 1985.
4. *PRO NED (Promotion of Non-Executive Directors)*, cited in note 5 below.
5. Bank of England, *The role of audit committees in banks*, Consultative paper prepared by the Banking Supervision Division, January 1987.
6. See note 3 above.
7. Sir Roy Griffiths, (Chairman), *National Health Service Management Engineering*, London: DHSS, 1983.
8. P.A. Samuelson, quoted in: J.K. Galbraith, *The age of uncer-*

160

tainty, London: Deutsch, 1977, p. 257.

Notes to 5. Richard Kearney, **The Spirit to Transform a People**
1. Tom Garvin, 'The Politics of Denial and Cultural Defiance', *The Irish Review*, 3, 1987.
2. Ibid.
3. We use the term 'radical pluralism' to distinguish the postmodern project from the arbitary or 'anything goes' pluralism of much liberal conservatism—an ideology which, as Marcuse and others have remarked, can easily collapse into a form of 'repressive tolerance'. See Herbert Marcuse, *Negations*, Beacon Press, 1968, and David Tracy, *Plurality and Ambiguity*, Harper and Row 1987. See Tracy, p. 90: 'Whenever any affirmation of pluralism . . . becomes simply a passive response to more and more possibilities, none of which shall ever be practiced, then pluralism demands suspicion. That kind is, as Simone de Beauvoir insisted, the perfect ideology for the modern bourgeois mind. Such a pluralism masks a genial confusion in which one tries to enjoy the pleasures of difference without ever committing oneself to any particular vision of resistance and hope. The great pluralists in the history of Western thought knew that any worthy affirmation of plurality was the beginning, but never the end, of a responsibly pluralistic attitude. There must be other criteria besides those of possibility and openness. There must be ethical-political criteria . . . any good pluralist should be able to discuss the differences between good, bad and downright awful interpretations'. Besides Tracy's outline of a postmodern hermeneutic of pluralism, one also finds a suggestive outline of a 'pluralist communicative ethic'—in contrast to the atomic individualism of liberal pluralism—in Hannah Arendt, *Between Past and Future* (Penguin 1977), pp. 163f.
4. Quoted by J.W. Foster, 'A Future for Irish Studies', *The Irish Review*, 3, 1987.
5. We might even speak here of *post-nationalism* in a sense analogous to the use of the term *post-modernism* by J.-F. Lyotard to mean a retrieval of modernity 'in its infancy'—thereby offering a constructive critique of its redundant or obsolescent aspects (see Lyotard, *The Postmodern Condition*, Manchester U.P. 1984). Similarly, post-

nationalism would mean advancing *beyond* nationalism, while retrieving what may have been progressive in its initial project e.g. the republican ideals of fraternity, liberty and equality together with the ecumenical dialogue between 'Catholic, Protestant and Dissenter'.

6. Alexis De Tocqueville, *Democracy in America*, ed. J.P. Mayer (Doubleday 1971), p. 508.

7. Pat Murphy, 'Open Letter' in *Circa*, no. 35, 1987, ed. L. Gibbons.

8. See Edna Longley's informative overview of these and other journals in her review article 'Regional Variations' in *The Irish Review*, 2, 1987.

9. Bob Quinn develops this argument in his book, *Atlantean*, Quartet, 1986.

10. To ensure that the new communications technology can contribute to a democratic expression of cultural regionalism, it is necessary to decentralise the means both of *production* (ownership and control) and of *distribution*. See Luke Gibbons's research on this subject commissioned by the EEC and presented to the 1983 conference in Cardiff on 'Film and Television in Celtic Countries'.

11. John Healy, 'Strasbourg Notebook', *Irish Times*, 20 Oct. 1987. The Hume Report (*On the Regional Problems of Ireland*, European Parliament Session Documents, English edn, 1987-88) on Regional Development criticises Ireland for its overcentralisation. While Northern Ireland is administered from 'above' (Belfast and London), the Republic suffers from the fact that too much sovereignty is concentrated in Dublin at the expense of the rest of the twenty-six counties. Hume argues for the creation of a new tier of elected regional authorities in Ireland with executive and planning powers (as well as strengthening the role of existing local authorities). This proposal for a new regional development policy—North and South—has been initially resisted by the respective nation-states (i.e. Britain and Ireland) whose finance departments have jealously guarded control over the EEC regional funds. Hume has argued that such a devolution of power to the regions would release local initiative and a new sense of purpose. It would also help to alleviate the present massive influx of citizens to the capital cities—Dublin now contains over a third of the entire

population of the Republic. The Hume proposal for decentralisation also points out that the new communications technology could be gainfully used to counteract the disadvantages of residing in 'remote' areas (i.e. anywhere outside of the capital). Aquaculture and forestry are seen as two areas where a new regional development fund might play a pivotal role. See *Irish Times*, 12 and 19 Oct. 1987: 'In essence the Hume Report recommends a revolution in the way Ireland is governed: it proposes to move power away from Dublin and to make the regions responsible for their future'. For a useful theoretical reflection on the concept of 'critical regionalism' see K. Frampton in *Postmodernism, ICA Documents*, 4. 1986, pp. 26-7. As applied to architecture, Frampton writes: 'By critical regionalism I do not mean any kind of specific style, nor of course do I have in mind any form of hypothetical vernacular revival, nor any kind of unreflected so-called spontaneous grass roots culture. Instead, I wish to employ this term in order to evoke a real and hypothetical condition in which a critical culture of architecture is consciously cultivated in a particular place, in express opposition to the cultural domination of hegemonic power. It is, in theory at least, the critical culture, which while it does not reject the thrust of modernisation, nonetheless resists being totally absorbed and consumed by it'.

12. See the *Report on Regional or Minority Languages in Europe*, drawn up by Herbert Kohn of West Germany for the Council of Europe (22nd Session, 20-22 Oct. 1987); and John Hume's paper on *The European Parliament and the Future of Lesser used Languages* in *The Lesser Used Languages of the European Community*, Comhar Teoranta, 1981. Hume stresses the positive advantages to be gained in the European context for the lesser-spoken languages, including of course the Irish language. See, finally, the *Contact Bulletin*, issued by the European Bureau for Lesser Used Languages and particularly the first number, Nov. 1983, where the Chairman, Dónall Ó Riagáin of *Gael-Linn*, outlines the positive implications of the resolutions passed by the European Parliament on a Community Charter of Regional Languages and Cultures and on a Charter of Rights of Ethnic Minorities. Finally, see the articles on European Regionalism, including 'Regionalism in Practice'

by Egon Weiderkamp, Chairman of the Committee for the Conference 'Europe of Regions' in *Regional Contact*, No. I, 1987, pp. 5-7.

13. It should be noted that the project for a postmodern Ireland has also been the subject of some suggestive analysis by a number of other commentators—in particular by the political economist Frank Barry, to whom I am indebted for several points in this essay (see his 'Between Tradition and Modernity' in *The Irish Review*, 2, 1987) and the theologian, Joseph O'Leary ('A Postmodern Theology for Ireland' in *Social Class and Irish Culture*, Derry 1987). See also Peter Neary's argument for a model of economic interdependence in 'The Failure of Economic Nationalism', *The Crane Bag*, Vol. 8, No. 1. 1984. Finally, see Desmond Fennell's influential writings on political and cultural regionalism in *Beyond nationalism*, Ward River, 1985, and other works.

14. This Voltaire vision was invoked by the French Foreign Minister, Jean-Bernard Raimond, in his opening address to the *International Symposium on European Cultural Identity* (Paris, 13-14 Jan. 1988). See the *Irish Times* report on this conference (22 Jan.) which saw proposals for several innovative measures regarding a new, enlarged and decentralised Europe of culture—comprising literary, intellectual and communicational/televisual dimensions and open to the 'other Europe' of the East in particular and to the non-European world in general.

15. See the numerous concrete measures passed or proposed in the European Parliament and Commission to create such a public sphere of communications culture in the European context, Part 2 of *Pour une Europe de la Culture* (published by the French Ministry of Foreign Affairs, Paris, 1987). These include, most notably, measures to establish a multi-lateral mechanism for supporting cinema and television co-productions between European countries, and the promotion of a European Cultural TV channel to be broadcast by satellite.